STARS OF SCIENCE
Innovators From All Over the Globe

This edition of *Stars of Science* is dedicated to:

The United Nations General Assembly's resolution designating 2003 to be the year of the 2,200th Anniversary of the statehood of The Kyrgyz Republic

Mairam Akaeva

STARS OF SCIENCE

Innovators From All Over the Globe

GLOBAL SCHOLARLY PUBLICATIONS
NEW YORK, NEW YORK AND PROVO, UTAH
2002

Copyright © 2002 by Mairam Akaeva

All rights reserved. No portion of this publication may be duplicated in any way without the expressed written consent of the publisher, except in the form of brief excerpts or quotations for review purposes.

Library of Congress Cataloging-in-Publication Data

Mairam Akaeva, *Stars of Science*

ISBN 1-59267-001-6

Published by Global Scholarly Publications
Brigham Young Unviersity, Provo, Utah
Distributed by Global Scholarly Publications
220 Madison Avenue
New York, New York 10016
Phone: (212) 679-6410   Fax: (212) 679-6424
E-mail: books@gsp-online.org
www.gsp-online.org

STARS OF SCIENCE

In this engaging and interesting book a well known author of books for children, Professor Mairam Akaeva, tells about outstanding scientists of the past and present. Each of them had his or her own way of learning the truth. Sometimes it was a hard one, filled with unique and unexpected adventures. This made victories that crowned their remarkable labors in the name of human progress even more precious.

*Translated into English from original Russian
by Ilyas Bekbolotov, M.A.*

Publisher's Acknowledgement

A treasure trove of the stories of historic scientific innovators worldwide, this wonderful book depicts scientists as paradigms of the power of the creative mind to shape nature in ways that serve our civilization. From Plato toNasir Khosrow, from Confucius to Thomas Edison, and from Euclid to Harvey Fletcher, all great thinkers have equated knowledge with power. Both in its practical and its theoretical modes, knowledge is indeed the way of salvation.

The perspective of this book is enriched by the diverse national origins of the scientific stars that the author chooses to depict, and by the global impact of their innovations. The blending of these two themes is suggestive of the unique gifts of the author's nation, the Kyrgyz Republic. The Kyrgyz Republic is a country where people with diverse nationalities live in harmony and peace, at the heart of the ancient Silk Road - the age-old route toward free trade and global peace.

The gifted author of this book is a winner of several international prizes for her successful efforts to educate the young in both computer technology and the history of science. Single handedly she has championed the cause of bringing computer technology and scientific education to rural parts of her country, enabling the young to reach for the stars of science and bless the global village with their hearts and minds.

The original Russian edition and the first English translation of this book were acclaimed in Central Asia and the Middle East. With appreciation, we salute Mairam Akaeva, the First Lady of the Kyrgyz Republic. Through her tireless efforts on charitable projects in education, she herself has become a graceful paradigm for mothers, scientists, and educators worldwide.

Parviz Morewedge, Ph.D.
Director, Global Scholarly Publications
A subsidiary of The Foundation
 for Interreligious Diplomacy

Charles Randall Paul, Ph.D.
President of The Foundation for
 Interreligious Diplomacy
New York and Utah

The privilege of being a genius is that life never becomes routine.

- James Lowell

He laughed when people called him genius; "Nonsense!" he said, "the secret of my genius is my hard work, determination, and common sense."

- Thomas Edison

Contents

Forward 1
Pythagoras 9
Confucius 35
Archimedes 63
Avicenna 73
Leonardo da Vinci 81
Johannes Kepler 97
Mikhailo Lomonosov 109
Jean Le Rond D'Alembert 127
Michael Faradei 143
Sofia Kovalievskaya 153
Ernest Rutherford 163
Srinivasa Ramanujan 181
Konstantin Kuzmich Yudakhin 193
Isa Akhunbaev 201
Euclid 209
Blaise Pascal 213
Bibliography 217

From the Author
"A Magic and Intense Passion"

Do you know, my dear friends, that science is one of the most exciting activities in the world? For people genuinely interested in the matter, science can provide the highest gratification, and moments of scientific accomplishment can turn out to be the most intense moments in one's life. Yet one has to work hard for the sake of those precious moments. The inventor Thomas Edison, who surprised the world with his inventions in the area of electricity in the 19th century, summarized in one sentence the challenges faced by the explorers of the unpredictable laws of nature. "Genius amounts to one percent inspiration and ninety-nine percent hard work," he said

Once you have become familiar with the heroes of this book, dear curious reader, you will agree with Edison's words. Who knows, maybe some day, if you are not afraid to devote your life to science, and take the road of the exploration of the unknown, you could also become like the heroes in the chapters of this book.

I am often asked why I chose to tell the stories of scientists of different periods and countries, including Kyrgyzstan. What motivated me to write about the scientific achievement of completely different people, united only by the fact that they are all geniuses of humankind?

In order to answer this question, I must remember my happy years as a student. They are now gone forever, but they gave me the unique chance to live in one of the most poetic cities of the world: Leningrad (now Saint-Petersburg). I remember sitting in a classroom in the prestigious university, and I remember Fyodor Litvin, who was a remarkable scientist, as well as an inspired professor; a specialist of mechanics, and physics; and a lyric poet, all at once! He was living proof that physics and poetry are actually compatible. Litvin was able to combine both talents brilliantly, and he could teach a difficult subject with a magic passion.

Fyodor Litvin's seemingly irrelevant tangents during lectures were actually brilliant when I understood them later. Thanks to his "improvisations" we students were able to understand very difficult aspects of science. For example, Fyodor Litvin would interrupt his explanation of mechanics by saying, "Let me tell you now about Leonardo da Vinci and his immortal piece, the Mona Lisa." Then he would stand, telling the story with great inspiration. On his tangent our professor would give us a great amount of information about the life and creations of Leonardo da Vinci, making us enthusiastic about his discoveries. Listening to his tangents we sometimes felt what it would be like to live during the Renaissance, among masters of science and art, and we sometimes felt what it would be like to jump into 18th century France, and face the burning eyes of Jean le Rond d'Alambert, the brilliant mathematician.

Out of sheer curiosity, we were proud to know that Niccolo Tartaglia, the Italian scientist and encyclopedist, was the lumping son of a poor family, or that Evariste Galois, the brilliant mathematician, died in a duel at the age of 20, or that Pierre Laplace, the founder of celestial mechanics, had to serve as Interior Minister for the dictatorial Napoleon! It was during those years that I developed a taste for the lives of the great scientists.

I soon became convinced that they could serve as role models not only for me, but for others, who wanted to motivate themselves for hard work in the field of science. Regardless of how different their lives were, all of the scientists in these pages were hard workers. The outstanding physicist Isaac Newton said, "Genius is about work." There isn't much to add to these words. Of course, not everyone is born with such gifts from Mother Nature, but I am strongly convinced that any of us can make the best of our skills and strive to become a genius.

After I graduated from Leningrad Technology University, I became a professor myself. Of course, I want my young and impulsive students to be inspired by a rather difficult subject - the theory of mechanics and machines - and to forget about everything else. Remembering my professor's lectures, I always try to tell my students about the private life of the great scientists of our civilization who brought real contributions to human progress through their intelligence and determination. That is how this book was born.

Mairam Akaeva.

Common wisdom considers science to be a collective undertaking. This is especially true for huge modern day labs and institutions, where armies of researchers are tinkering with an ever-growing arsenal of sophisticated high-tech instruments. However, the most remarkable feature of the inner kitchen of science was, and still is the role played by a few individuals, whose geniuses tower over the crowd and carry the torch of new groundbreaking ideas. Such is the enigmatic nature of human intellectual potential, enabling a few of the blessed to do what in the eyes of the rest looks like a sheer miracle. The legacy of these great scientists and investors transforms our lives, teaches us to understand nature, and arms us with the tools to advance civilization.

No matter how grateful this generation of man is for the legacy left by the Masters of Science, one of the sad ironies of today's reality is how little men on the street know about them and their unusual and often heroic lives. Perhaps because of our market culture, the mass media and entertainment industry are promoting, especially for young audiences, the images of celebrities — pop singers, and movie and sport stars. With the revolutionary explosion of information and communication technologies we need as never before, genuine food for thought. We need noble words for true geniuses of creative intellectual endeavors to complement and strengthen the call for an urgent upgrade in science education on every level.

This essay on "stars of science" by Mairam Akaeva precisely belongs to this type of literature. It is capable of inspiring readers with great images of the heroes of science, and extraordinary stories of their lives and outstanding discoveries. The author carries us through a gallery of brilliant scientists from ancient Greece to China and India. The geography of major scientific schools and discoveries makes us feel the oneness of the human family, notwithstanding the religious, political, or cultural differences.

The names in these chapters are familiar to many, since Dr. Akaeva has presented everyone's school years in a new light, with delicately selected details and episodes. From the distant epoch of antiquity, the reader may discover Pythagoras, who preceded the great founders of exact sciences: Euclid and Archimedes. Pythagoras, known to anyone for his legendary theorem on triangles, appears now as broad-minded thinker and philosopher, and even an outstanding public figure. Another of Pythagoras' important qualities, his talent as a teacher, is eloquently depicted in the book. His pupils and followers carried and advanced his ideas for several generations.

A thousand years later the titans of the Islamic Renaissance followed up on the deeds of the Great Greeks. At that time Europe was still in the stiff embraces of the Dark Ages, with very little left from the legacy of Plato and Aristotle. Muslim thinkers carried their baton. Central Asia (Kyrgyzstan - the home country of Mairam Akaeva - is in the heart of this region) provided a home for a number of them. The author focused on the dominating figure of Avicenna (Ibn Sina). He absorbed the best from the Greeks and established a new standard in many areas of intellectual activity. His "Canons of Medicine" became indispensable for every doctor over the centuries. The universality of his interests and scope of outstanding contribution was not limited by sciences. He served as an advisor to several rulers during a Golden Age in Central Asia. This was an enormously productive period in the history of Muslim civilization. It proves that Moderate Islam is not an enemy of progress. This message is becoming especially important now.

The true genius rarely confines his creative nature in a narrow area of interests. The life story of Leonardo Da Vinci is the best testament to this rule. The famous enigmatic smile of Mona Lisa is only one of his magnificent artistic masterpieces, and he was ahead of his time by several centuries when he invented machines of the future technology age, like the helicopter and the submarine.

The life of all great scientists involves uncompromised dedication and service to their profession. Far from a continuous celebration, it is more often a struggle to find the means to do their work, or provide for their family. It requires real ingenuity, and entrepreneurship to deal with the sober realities of being a professional scientist. The great astronomer Kepler taught himself to play the role of astrologer in order to please the royalty of the medieval European courts. Sophia Kovalevsky, a prominent Russian mathematician of the late 19th century, had to invent and implement the whole scenario of a fictitious marriage in order to break through tight parental control and gain the right to become the scientist she wanted to be.

Often the truly revolutionary discoveries require great scientists to have enormous civil courage in order to confront the hostile ignorance of contemporaries. However, the very subject of science always serves as a driving force throughout their lives. There is no greater joy or satisfaction than the moment of revelation or discovery (even if it is only a small step in the progress and advancement of knowledge).

It is not surprising how masterfully Mairam Akaeva expresses the way the scientists in this book felt about their work. Albert Einstein once remarked, "... duty and joy are one and the same." The passion with which Mairam Akaeva tells us these stories, she developed during her own years as a student, and throughout her career in science. She was greatly influenced by prominent professors and teachers, as well as by the intellectual atmosphere in St. Petersburg (then Leningrad), the genuine cradle of Russian science. I firmly believe that the readers of this wonderful book will share Dr. Akaeva's passion and excitement.

Professor R. Z. Sagdeev, Ph.D
University of Maryland, USA.

PYTHAGORAS
(576-496 BC)

An ancient Greek philosopher and scientist, Pythagoras was the founder of the Pythagorean philosophy on world harmony. According to this philosophy, numbers are the key to nature's secrets.

> "Two things make a man godly: a life dedicated to social welfare, and a life dedicated to justice."

Pythagoras, called Pythagoras of Samos by his contemporaries and followers, is probably the most well known figure in the history of science. Generations of school students prove his Pythagorean Theorem in geometry class, and even if they don't remember it years after graduating from school, they still recall the joke about Pythagoras' trousers.

Today Pythagoras is remembered not only as a talented scientist, but also as an extremely strong personality. He was a great philosopher, a reformer of religion and esthetics, a master of thoughts, a supporter of his own Pythagorean ethic, and an influential politician. Pythagoras had a mind that could be compared to those of Buddha and Confucius, his greatest contemporaries. His teachings were based on common sense, as well as the assurance that nature's secrets could be read. As a result, his students and supporters adopted them as a religion.

Twenty five centuries ago in a legendary and almost fairy-tale Ancient Greece, when human conscienceness was still influenced by mythology and magic, Pythagoras opened the first scientific school, spurring the beginning of a new, philosophical conception of the world. All of humankind should be grateful for the sudden advances in the progress of mathematics, physics, astronomy and musicology, that followed the opening of Pythagoras' school. At that time, his students considered him to be a semi-God, and his jealous rivals named him a charlatan. Unfortunately, not a single work by Pythagoras survived. His ideas, discoveries, and visions were only transmitted to us through the works of his followers, including Diogenes, Laertius,

Porphyrius, and Iamblichus, who wrote in the 3rd century BD about the Great Greeks.

Pythagoras was still a very popular figure after his death. Coins were created with his portrait engraved on them in the city of Abder in the year 430 BC, fifty years after his death. Abder was in no way related to Pythagoras's life, and only the portraits of rulers and military leaders were engraved on coins at that time (the tradition of engraving portraits of scientists and philosophers came later). Almost a century after Pythagoras' death his genius was still a matter of debate in the schools of Plato and Aristotle. Pythagoras was also the first man in human history to have a book dedicated to him. A student of Pythagorean philosophy, Democritus from Abder, expressed his admiration for Pythagoras of Samos in his book.

Pythagoras' fame made him an inspiration for legends in his time, and as a result his name survived the centuries. It was because of his radiant star quality that historians were able to retrace the life of this great man.

"Young people must dedicate all their lives to common sense."

According to legend, Pythagoras was born on the island of Samos in the Aegean Sea, on the shore of Asia Minor. Therefore, his biographers called him Pythagoras of Samos. Pythagoras' father, Mnesarchus, was a talented artist and stone sculptor who used his skills to earn money. Although he came from a noble family, Mnesarchus did not inherit much wealth. According to some sources, Parthenis, Pythagoras' mother, was from the Achean family that founded the island of Samos.

When the young couple was expecting their first child, they spoke to the Delphi oracle. The oracle predicted the birth of a son, "who will be famous for centuries because of his works, beautiful as Apollo, and wise as Pythias." When the child was born, the happy father brought him to the priest of the temple and asked for Apollo's protection. Parthenis followed the ancient traditions and took the name of Pythiada, in honor of Apollo of Pythias, and their son was called Pythagoras, which means Pythias' predictions. Some ancient historians believed that Pythagoras was not a name, but a nickname given to the small boy as he spoke the truth from his earliest age, just as Apollo of Pythias did.

The little boy was beautiful, and he soon developed extraordinary skills. Pythagoras' father gave the talented child all the necessary tools to make the oracle's prediction come true. The temple became Pythagoras' first school, and the priest his first teacher. Later, Hermodamas, a descendant of Kreophylius of Samos, took over the education of the boy. It is believed that Kreophylius also took into his house the old Homer, and saved all of his poems for future generations. To train his memory, Hermodamas taught the young Pythagoras the poems of the Iliad and the Odyssey. Strong impressions were made on his young, developing soul by the images of the gods, and the poetic descriptions of the heroes' strength, courage, strong will to fight against life's disasters, joy in the beauty of their homelands, and joy in love.

Hermodamas gave Pythagoras the basics of music and painting, taught him to love nature, and inspired him to seek out nature's secrets. "Your senses come from nature," said Hermodamas, "therefore nature should be the first subject of your studies!"

Pherecydes of Syros, a poet and philosopher, also took part in the education of the young Pythagoras. He was delighted by his student's curiosity. "Go on a journey," he once told the young boy, "this is the only way to satisfy your desire for knowledge. Travelling improves a man and opens to him the doors of wisdom."

At that time the island of Samos was governed by Polycrates, and even though the island lacked natural resources, the citizens were not poor, because arts and craftsmanship were blossoming. Eupalin, an outstanding engineer, made a tunnel to bring water to the city from a mountainous lake. The tunnel of Samos was called one of the world's wonders, and when archeologists discovered it, they could hardly believe such a project took place 2,500 years ago.

A talented philosopher or craftsman could have easily found his place under the enlightened ruler Polycrates, but a free spirit needs more space.

"The beginning is half the work."

For Samos' inhabitants, all the roads to the world went through Milet, the Ionian metropolis, but the young Pythagoras was particularly eager to visit that island because the scientist Phales, famous all over Greece, lived there. Phales was considered the top sage in Ancient Greece in those days. It is believed that when the Greek people wanted to offer a golden tripod to the wisest of men, the oracle proposed Phales, but because Phales was a modest man, he passed the gift to the second wisest man in the country, who then passed it on to the third wisest, and so on. In the end, the tripod returned to Phales.

Phales was a great mathematician and astronomer. He was the first to measure the height of the Egyptian pyramids from their shadow, and he was also able to predict solar eclipses. Like a real sage, he lived alone, and avoided stress. The young Pythagoras doubted the old sage would agree to postpone his research for the sake of a young visitor, but his doubts were mistaken. The meeting did take place. Wise men, unlike despots, are not afraid of young and daring spirits. They see in the young the continuation of their work and ideas.

In Milet Pythagoras attended Phales' lessons, as well as lessons by Phale's student and colleague, Anachsimander, who was also a famous scientist, geographer, and astronomer. Anachsimander was famous for having invented the first astrological instrument, a solar clock, and for drawing the first map of the world.

Phales intuitively understood that the young Pythagoras was restless, and advised him to go to Egypt to carry on his education in Memphis. This advise came as no surprise to Pythagoras, because according to all of his contemporaries, Egypt was the center of wisdom. Compared to the ancient Egyptian civilization, the Greeks viewed themselves as children. They were overwhelmed by the miracles of Egyptian architecture. For the Greeks living in the 5th century BC, the pyramids were as ancient as the ruins of the Acropolis are for us.

The brightest scientists, philosophers, poets, and singers in all of Greece went to Egypt to improve their knowledge. The country was visited by Orpheus, Eudocle, Democritus, and many others, for whom life meant studying. Egypt was also named the motherland of mathematics (at least Aristotle had no doubts about this, 200 years later). Yet Egyptian mathematics was merely a practical science, serving the needs of counting (arithmetic) and measurement of the ground (geometry). Aristotle's student, Eudem of Rhodes, wrote in his work, *History of Geometry*, "Geometry was invented by the Egyptians for measuring the ground. It was needed because every flood of the Nile destroyed the frontiers between pieces of land." If the Nile took away a piece of land, the civil servants had to remeasure the land so that the landowner would pay taxes according to the real size of the land.

Pythagoras, of course, intended to reach the heights of Egyptian mathematics, but he was also attracted by the Egyptian gods. Knowledge of Egyptian gods was holy, and therefore kept secret by the Egyptians, but besides that there was a language barrier that prevented the Greeks from obtaining certain knowledge from the Egyptians. Pythagoras managed to surmount both of these obstacles. Diogenes Laertius, quoting Antiphon's book, *About Extraordinary People,* writes that Pythagoras was given a letter of recommendation for Pharaoh Amasis by Polycrates, who stated that Pythagoras had mastered the Egyptian language. Thanks to Amasis' protection, Pythagoras was gradually able to become an equal member of the cast of priests who were familiar with all the secrets of Egyptian temples. Needless to say, by the age of forty, called Akme in Greek and considered the peak of one's abilities, Pythagoras had become one of the most educated humans of his time.

"The cup of life would be too sweet without sour tears."

According to the ancient biographer Iamblichus, Pythagoras spent 22 years in Egypt before something terrible happened. Pharaoh Amasis died, and his successor refused to pay taxes to the Persian king, Kambis. War was declared, and the Persians destroyed everything in their way, including Egyptian holy temples. They entered temples, destroyed altars, killed some priests, and took others hostage, including Pythagoras. For an independent intellectual like Pythagoras, this was a tragedy.

In those days, a captive could enjoy a normal life if he had a special talent, skill, or knowledge. According to historians, Pythagoras spent his two years in Babylonian captivity learning the secrets of the Persian priests. Babylon was an ancient metropolis at the crossroads of many trade routes. It gathered together an incredible number of nationalities, traditions, habits, and languages. Many legends across the centuries tell us about Babylon's achievements in engineering, science, and art. These legends were proved to be true at the end of the 19th century, by the work of the German archeologist Robert Koldewei in areas surrounding Baghdad. His expeditions made extraordinary discoveries, including an underground tunnel in Semiramis palace, the basement of Babylon Tower, and an official road that improved on modern roads. Even at the beginning of the third millennium we can still be surprised!

With his constant desire for knowledge, Pythagoras opened new horizons for himself in Babylon. Apuleius writes in his *Florides* that the Chaldeans opened new secrets to the talented captive. They taught him the science of astrology. They explained to him that medicine is made of air, earth, and sea. Pythagoras mixed his Greek philosophy with the Brahman teachings concerning exercises for the body and soul at different ages, and also the Brahman teachings concerning punishments for the dead.

At the same time, Pythagoras mastered the latest knowledge in Eastern arithmetic, geometry, astronomy and medicine. His curious mind never stopped learning, and that attracted the attention of all of his contemporaries. The Persian king Hystaps heard about the great Greek, and finally, after Pythagoras had been 35 years away from his home, he was granted his freedom. Pythagoras turned 60, gathered all the scientific achievements of his time, joined his knowledge of Egypt and the East, and brought this precious treasure back to his homeland - to Greece, and the island of his childhood and youth, Samos.

> ## "Learn about people. It is easier and more useful to learn about people than to learn about gods."

He was greeted in his homeland by total desolation; the former prosperity was gone without a single trace. As a result of wars with the Persians, Samos became a remote, underdeveloped province. Most of the gifted people fled from the barbarians to Southern Italy. The colonies they founded there, in Syracuse, Agrigente, and Croton, were part of an area that became known as *Great Greece*. Pythagoras had no choice but to move to Croton. It was not like the Samos of his youth, but it was not bad, and Pythagoras decided to found a philosophical school there.

It may seem incredible that an immigrant from faraway Samos could win so much support in Croton, with discourses as his only way to gain popularity, but Pythagoras did. His first speech was in the local gymnasium. It was a discourse on ethics and respect for elders. Within a matter of days it brought Pythagoras phenomenal fame throughout the city. After that, whenever the white-haired sage appeared on the street in his white clothes, he was immediately surrounded by a throng of supporters. It seemed that his positive energy attracted people's attention, and his moderate, wise words opened their hearts.

The elders of the city became preoccupied with Pythagoras as well, so they asked him to speak for them. When Pythagoras gave them his speech on justice and harmony, they were overwhelmed by his talent and energy. This speech was Pythagoras' first step toward moral and political power in Croton. The enthusiasm he caused was so great that women broke the law preventing them from taking part in gatherings. A young woman called Tano fell in love with Pythagoras, and soon became his wife.

The political situations in Croton and other cities of Great Greece were tense because of a growing social gap, and to make things even worse, the inhabitants of the neighboring city of Sybaris were living in luxury. It was at this time that Pythagoras delivered a bright speech on moral perfection and knowledge of the world. It was so convincing that the people of Croton unanimously voted him the moral censor, and the spiritual father of the city.

This burden did not frighten the sage. Drawing from the things he studied during his journeys, and selecting the best ideas from various religions and beliefs, Pythagoras created his own bright and positive religion, aimed toward world harmony. The center of this religion was the conviction that all beings, including nature, man, and the cosmos, were connected, and all people were equal in the face of eternity. Pythagoras believed that nature and God were one. He believed that in order to have a full understanding of God, one must know nature. "The cosmos is larger than you can ever imagine," Pythagoras told his students. "He is a living celestial being, and He never dies, being the beginning and the reason for this world order. May this order be your god, and may you serve Him with all your heart! Order is the union of all things and nature lives in this order."

The teachings Pythagoras obtained from Egyptian priests, and the rituals he mastered with the Persian sages, gave his speeches a special force.. Croton's inhabitants began going to Pythagoras for healing. He purified their souls and cleaned their hearts, filling their minds with bright truth. Just as the ploughed ground awaits the seed, the people awaited his wise words.

"Run away from smart tricks; get rid of pain with fire, iron, or any weapon; get rid of bad thoughts of luxury; free the city of the problems of family disputes; get rid of unnecessary things!" he said.

In his *Golden Verses*, the philosopher developed his moral principles, leading lost souls to perfection and harmony. In these verses he expressed eternal human values, which are still relevant today, 2,500 years later. Here is some of his advise:

"Do not run after happiness, for it is always within yourself."

"Live simply."

"Measure your wishes, weigh your thoughts, choose your words."

"Accept your lot, whatever it is, and don't complain."

"Never do what you do not know, but learn everything that can be learned, and then you will have a worthy life."

"First, try to be wise and educated. Then you will be free to do other things."

According to legend, after Pythagoras gave his first lessons he had 2,000 students living in a huge community with their wives and children. The community was based on Pythagoras' rules and regulations. The Pythagorean Union, made up mostly of the younger supporters of Pythagoras, was the main force of the community of students. The Union gathered all the energy of young minds and hearts, and soon became the leading spiritual center of the city.

The Pythagoreans played an essential role in the war against the city of Sybaris, which was then the leading force of the entire Appenin Peninsula. The defeat of the Sybarites gave political power to the Pythagoreans in Croton. As a result, the ideas of the Union crossed the borders of the city and conquered many more cities of Great Greece.

New Pythagorean clubs were founded all over Great Greece. Diogenes Laertius wrote in categorical terms about these events. According to him, Pythagoras imposed his rules on Southern Italy, and became the top political leader. He dedicated an important part of his long and busy life to politics, and the education of politicians.

Pythagoras also taught his students to take an interest in politics. One of the principles of the Union said, "Always and everywhere, do only what is useful and beneficial for general harmony, for nature, and for human society." Still, the most important value that united the Pythagorean brotherhood was "the aspiration to beauty and being useful." Pythagoras taught that a real love of beauty is reflected in a love for nature and science.

For Pythagoras, the Union meant a lot. He gained not only devoted followers, but valuable students to whom he could pass on the precious knowledge he accumulated during his long journeys. He also found people who could carry on his research. Pythagoras started gathering his students in his house, and the first scientific school was born from these discussions and conversations. The school had a tremendous influence on Pythagoras' contemporaries, as well as future generations.

Diogenes Laertius stated that the school founded by the philosopher lasted nine generations. This is probably an exaggeration, but it is true that the school formed scientists, politicians and community leaders, who had a determining influence on the cultural and political development of many cities around the Mediterranean for more than a hundred years.

The biographer Iamblichus, andardent supporter of the

sage, wrote about the Pythagorean school a few centuries later in his work, *The Life of Pythagoras*. According to him, the school had an unusual selection of students and an unusual method of teaching. Pythagoras gave as much importance to moral qualities as to intellectual skills. He studied the character of candidates, and gave them a test of silence. Iamblichus states that sometimes this test lasted for five years. The ritual to join the Pythagorean brotherhood was secret, and divulging its secrets was severely punished. According to Apuleius, the first task on the road to wisdom was to master "the words, the very words poets call flying birds, behind the white wall of teeth." In other words, he believed that wisdom starts when you think, instead of talking nonsense.

Men and women were both accepted as members of the Pythagorean Union, and neither were given any privileges for having riches, or special knowledge. The only requirements for the Union were strong intellectual and moral qualities. According to Iamblichus, anyone joining the Pythagorean Union gave up his or her property for common use. Despite their cohesion, the students of Pythagoras were strictly separated into different echelons. The most gifted students, called the mathematicians (the discoverers), and the less talented students, called the akousmatics (the listeners) learned separately. Very often the teacher used a language of symbols and expressions to protect holy knowledge from listeners who were mere passersby, and not initiators.

The main Pythagorean symbol was the pentagram, or Pythagorean star, a figure embodying the famous Pythagorean properties: arithmetic, geometric, harmonic, and golden. Probably because of its mathematical qualities, the Pythagoreans selected the star not only as their emblem, but as a symbol of health and life. The pentagram became a secret sign, allowing

Pythagoreans to recognize each other. Legend has it that once when a Pythagorean member was dying far away from their home, in a stranger's house, and they couldn't afford to pay the owner for their burial, they asked the owner to draw a pentagram on the wall of the house, facing the road. "If fate brings a Pythagorean to this land," said the agonized Pythagorean, " he or she will stop here and thank you for your goodness." Indeed it happened that a few years later another Pythagorean saw the symbol of the Brotherhood, found out the whole story from the owner of the house, and paid him back.

The Pythagorean Union was a closed organization that allowed a community of people sharing the same scientific and philosophic knowledge and opinions to build their shared lives in a particular way. Pythagoras worked out a special daily routine for himself and his students. They would wake up while it was still dark, and go to the sea to meet the sunrise. For the inhabitants of Croton, located on the eastern bank of the Appenin Peninsula, the sun would rise from the sea, and this beautiful vista inspired the souls of the Pythagoreans. Still fresh from their early morning, the Pythagorean brothers and sisters would then discuss the issues of the day, practice gymnastics, and have breakfast, all in the holy wood. Pythagoras himself liked to meet the new day playing the lyre and chanting Homeric verses. The old man was tired of crowds, and preferred the company of two or three students. The whole day would then be dedicated to science and discussion. Towards the evening there would be a common walk, and a swim in the sea. After dinner the gods would be honored, and at the end of the day there would be a reading. A youngster would read, and an elder would comment on the text.

The sage insisted that there were two moments in a day that a person had to devote to thinking. These were right before they fell asleep, and right before they got out of bed. It was essential to look back and judge what was accomplished during the day, at night, and it was essential to look forward to what awaited in the new day, in the morning.

A real pedagogue, Pythagoras introduced exercises to improve intellectual capacities among his students. With these exercises, the Pythagoreans trained their attention, their memory, and their analytical skills. The teacher also encouraged an exercise in which the events of the previous day were recalled and analyzed, in order to improve students memories, and at the same time, educate them morally. Every evening when they practiced this exercise, the Pythagoreans learned to appreciate the power of their words and actions, and at the same time, they strengthened their mechanical memory and logic.

Another essential element in the Pythagorean education was the cleansing of the soul by music. Great importance was given to musical education. It was believed that certain melodies and rhythms could influence human morals and passions, and therefore help to purify and harmonize the spiritual forces.

The brotherhood also paid tremendous attention to food. Pythagoreans had no doubt that different sorts of food had different influences on the soul. Pythagoras taught that meat destroyed the spiritual balance and caused disorder in thoughts, and for this reason all the members of the organization were vegetarian. Moreover, the Pythagoreans considered that extreme thinness or obesity were signs of an unhealthy life-style, so they were very concerned with their own physical aspect. Because they were concerned with universal harmony, a person's health had tremendous meaning. As a result, the students of Pythagoras paid great attention to medicine and the improvement of the body. It is well known that the school of Croton created the foundation for ancient medicine.

The term "kalokagathia" was invented by the Pythagorean school. It refers to the Greek ideal of a man, including beauty, health, intelligence, and spiritual qualities. Their care for the harmony of the spiritual and the physical brought outstanding results for the Pythagoreans. Many of them were Olympic winners. The six-time Olympic champion, Milo, was a student of Pythagoras. Phail, who jumped 55 Delphic lengths (16.3 meters), was also a Pythagorean.

Many sayings have survived the ages from the time of the Pythagoreans, such as "The last of the Crotonians is the first of Greeks." The expression "strong Crotonian" was used in stories at that time to refer to the highest degree of physical strength. Kalogathia remained an ultimate reference in Ancient Greece, and was passed on to the Romans. "A healthy mind in a healthy body," is a saying that refers to the Greek ideal.

"If you are asked about what makes a good man, give the answer: 'Wisdom in actions.'"

The whole Pythagorean brotherhood had to fulfill ethical requirements. They had to respect their elders, and their parents, cherish friendship, respect justice for all, including animals, and honor agreements. These rules were the basis of Pythagorean ethics. Philosophy, which in Ancient Greek means "love for wisdom," had many different aspects for the Pythagoreans. The love for wisdom included the desire to obtain knowledge, to master the mind, and to be a gentleman.

According to legend, Pythagoras himself invented the word "philosophy". Once he met the great sage, Leont, the ruler of the city of Fliuntum, and Leont asked him what science he mastered best.

"None," replied Pythagoras, " I am a mere philosopher."

"And what does philosopher mean?" asked Leont, for whom the word was new.

"One can compare life to the Olympic Games," explained the old Pythagoras. "One participates in the arena for the sake of fame and honors, another comes to discuss matters of business, and another comes just to watch. The same applies to life; some serve glory, and others money, but a small number ignore these matters and study nature, putting truth above all else. They call themselves 'philosophers' (lovers of wisdom)," he explained, "but not 'sophers' (sages), as only gods master wisdom, and man can only try."

The modesty of this great man honors his memory.

Pythagoras also used the word "cosmos" to mean universe, for the first time. It used to refer to "order, perfection, beautiful machine" in Ancient Greek. Pythagoras wanted to emphasize the world's order, relevance, symmetry, and godly beauty. For Pythagoreans, order and symmetry were beautiful, and chaos and asymmetry destroyed harmony. They were convinced that the beauty of the "macro-cosmos," or the universe, was accessible only to those who lived right, having wisely organized their "microcosmos". The Pythagorean life-style was therefore not simply empty words, but - one might say - a high, cosmic goal to bring the harmony of the world to the earthly human life.

> **"To avoid worrying about what people think of you, do what you consider fair. Be indifferent to critics and flatterers."**

Of course, concrete scientific subjects were also taught in the school of the "greatest Hellenistic sage," as Herodotus named Pythagoras a century later. Pythagoras shared with his students the precious knowledge he accumulated during his journeys to Egypt and Babylon. The Pythagorean educational system included large programs in mathematics, astronomy, music, and medicine, and a serious course on politics (as politics was regarded as the main means to influence minds). The Pythagorean school formed outstanding mathematicians, historians, astronomers, politicians and statesmen, who were one hundred years ahead of the development of the science, culture, art, and political and social life in other Mediterranean cities. Pythagoras was a wise pedagogue and an enthusiastic scientist, and his students were no different.

Very soon, the Pythagorean school became famous beyond the borders of Great Greece. Pythagoras' students spread his ideas to all the cities of the Mediterranean, eventually allowing for friendly relations between former enemy cities. Porphyrius wrote that through his students, Pythagoras settled disputes "on all the roads of Italy and Sicily." The influence of Pythagoras' teachings on his contemporaries was huge. It is said that the tyrant Simichus gave up his power after spending some time with the Pythagoreans, and distributed his riches to his parents and citizens. Fame and wealth were irrelevant in the brotherhood, which cherished honor, intelligence, talent and a clear conscience. Such ideals shocked the minds and souls of many. At a time when tyrants were the typical model of rulers, propagating ideas that placed spiritual and intellectual qualities above everything else was dangerous.

Conflict began in Croton when it seemed that the Pythagoreans were at the peak of their political power, with Milo as their leader. Iamblichus writes that some opponents appeared among influential Crotonian citizens. The opposition was headed by Cylon, a man of a difficult and ambitious character. He had tried to enter the Union and master the knowledge of the happy few, but was denied membership. He decided to get revenge by starting a vigorous war against the Pythagoreans.

Events developed so fast, and with so much violence, that old Pythagoras had to move away to Metapontum. Having lost his life's work, and seen his supporters persecuted, he died there in bitterness, refusing to take food for forty days. Without the continuation of his teachings, the old philosopher had lost the meaning of his life.

In the mean time, the war between the Pythagoreans and the Cyloneans reached its peak. The Cyloneans burned down Milo's house while the Pythagoreans were gathered there. Many of them were unable to escape, and so died in the terrible fire. Many fled and settled in different parts of Ancient Greece, making the teachings of Pythagoras even more popular around the Mediterranean. All the knowledge and beliefs that were accumulated during their years spent with Pythagoras, which had previously been mentioned only in secret signs, began to be written down, in order to be transmitted to future generations.

"Accomplish great things without promising anything great."

The seeds of Pythagoras' knowledge were saved by his dedicated supporters, with very good results. The further development of science and philosophy after Pythagoras' death was still connected with Pythagoreans, through the famous mathematician Architus, who left Croton and opened his school in Tarentum, Archippus and Clinius who fled to Regium, and Philola and Lysis who settled in Thebes.

Throughout his years as a political force on earth, and even after his death, Pythagoras was seen not as a man, but as a legend. Pythagoreans used to say during Pythagoras' life that intelligent beings belong to three categories: Gods, humans, and the "ones similar to Pythagoras." The Pythagoreans claimed that their teacher could predict natural disasters such as earthquakes, and calm sea waves. They said that he had the power to stop epidemics. They even claimed that he warned them of the anti-Pythagorean wars - of the persecution and death.

In the eyes of simple citizens, the philosopher was simply a semi-god. They believed Pythagoras had a golden hip, and that once in Tyrenium he bit and killed a poisonous snake that had killed many citizens. Some reported that the Kas River once greeted the philosopher with, "Be happy, Pythagoras," in the same manner that the Ancient Greeks greeted each other. The very name of Pythagoras became a synonym for "miracle".

The real miracle was that Pythagoras brought knowledge to human kind at a time when rivers spoke, and the gods of Mount Olympus engaged in conversations with simple mortals. Diogenes Laertius said that Pythagoras was the first to introduce measurements and weights in Ancient Greece. Proclus called him the greatest mathematician of his time when he proved that the sum of the internal angles of a triangle were equal to the sum of two right-angles, and that the square of the length of the hypotenuse of a right triangle was equal to the sum of the squares of the legs (the famous Pythagorean theorem). The discovery of infinity, which challenged the Pythagorean theory of numbers and was therefore kept secret, is usually attributed to the head of the brotherhood.

Aristoxenus wrote in his work, *About Arithmetic*, that Pythagoras developed the science of arithmetic, liberating it from the burden of merchants. Proclus said that Pythagoras redesigned geometry, making it a free science by describing it abstractly, and researching it intellectually. Pythagoras and his students researched geometry systematically, not like a manual of agricultural instructions, but like a theoretical teaching about abstract geometric figures. All was based on measurements and logical proofs.

Geometry was applied in many practical fields. It was the first science shared with the world by a brother that left the Pythagoreans and entered the world of the non-initiated, and it became the most popular science of the time. In his *Life of Pythagoras*, Iamblichus wrote that geometry spread throughout the world because of the mistake of one of the brothers who lost the money of the community. After that, the Pythagoreans allowed him to regain the missing money using geometry. That is how geometry came to be known as Pythagoras' Betrayal. Soon after, it was used by the state to gather money.

As a mathematician, Pythagoras discovered the theory of proportions, and with his philosophical genius, and what we now see as incredible intuition, he stated, "All matters are numbers." This theory, which shocked all of his contemporaries, proves still to be true today. Today we all accept that mathematics is the key to understanding all the secrets of nature. Pythagoras proclaimed something else that seemed impossible in Ancient Greece. He said, "Numbers are the wisest things. Every thing does not start from numbers, but it is connected to numbers, as they contain order..." American mathematician and science historian M. Klein, wrote that Pythagoras' genius and intuition enabled the development of two theories which defined the development of all sciences. First, the theory that the basic rules sustaining the world can be expressed in the language of mathematics. Second, the theory that numbers connect all the elements of the universe, expressing the harmony and order of nature.

> "Truth must be seen naked. Let lies be covered with clothes."

Today, mathematics is often related to music. It is clear that Pythagoras also saw this connection when he used music to prove his theory that "all matters are numbers." According to Plutarch, Pythagoras denied the emotional aspect of music, and declared that music must be appreciated for the harmony which could be described in mathematical terms. Biographers wrote that Pythagoras' idea of a numerical basis for the universe was born out of empiric and not logical ideas. Pythagoras was passing by a blacksmith one day, when he noticed that different hits of the hammer resulted in different sounds, depending on the hammer's weight. Studying the problem, he found that the echo depended on the weight of the hammer, and transposing the problem to strings, he discovered the connection between a string's thickness and length, and the quality of the sound.

His experiments proved that harmony could be expressed using mathematics. Harmony takes place when the length of a string vibrates in proportions close to the following numbers: $2/1$, $3/2$, $4/3$ and so on. Thus, the law of proportions resolves musical harmony into mathematical terms. Other experiments Pythagoras did on musical tones developed into theories of music and acoustics, and resulted in the creation of the famous Pythagorean scale, which laid the foundations of musical culture. (It is worth noting that music was also researched by Euclid, Clavius, Ptolemes, Johannes Kepler, Gottfried Leibniz, Leonard Euler, and many others.)

The Pythagoreans were overwhelmed with the discovery that music and harmony could be translated into mathematics, because it meant that an element of nature could be described by numbers! No wonder the numbers 1, 2, 3, and 4, called the tetrad and used for the basis of euphony in music, were given magic attributions and declared godly. Having discovered harmonious intervals, the Pythagoreans saw the tetrad as the basis for deciphering all the secrets of the universe. A point has one dimension, a line has two, a surface three, and a volume four. At the same time, one symbolizes the spirit of all beings, two symbolizes the material atom, three is a symbol of the living world, and four represents the visible and invisible world. The sum of 1-4 makes 10, the symbol of everything in the universe. The oath of the brotherhood of Pythagoras said, "I give oath in the name of the tetrad given to our souls, as that is the source and the root of ever prospering nature!"

Pythagoreans were accused of numerical mysticism because they strongly believed that they could describe the spiritual world with numbers. They thought justice and equality could be easily expressed with mathematics. They considered 9 the symbol of loyalty, and 8 the mark of death.

Certain numbers were adored by the Pythagoreans. The cult of seven was probably adopted by the Greeks from Babylon. Thirty-six was a particularly admired number, because the cube of the first digit, three, was the same as the sum of the two digits, three and six. The brothers believed that the universe was built on such numbers, and as a result, the oath based on 36 was the most powerful one. For us it may seem naive that the Pythagoreans strongly believed in numbers as the only way to truth, yet one must not forget that all this took place when scientific knowledge was just being born.

Obviously Pythagoras was the first to discover abstract knowledge. He told his students that the mind, and not the senses, brought real knowledge, and he advised them to switch from physical thoughts to abstract mathematical thoughts that allowed man to understand eternal truth. The name of Pythagoras is also connected to astronomy and cosmology. Historians claim that he was the first to notice the bent position of the Zodiac, and the first to calculate the length of the "great year," the intervals among the positions of planets. Pythagoras' astronomy was purely abstract, yet its rationality allowed Pythagoras and his successors to make correct estimations about the structure of the universe. They could not prove it, but based on primary symmetry and harmony, they claimed that the shape of the planets were like balls, and that they revolved around themselves.

There is one more legend about Pythagoras' role in astronomy. Ancient sources claim that Pythagoras, who had miraculous attributes, was able to hear the sound waves of stars, and listen to the music of spheres. Porphyrius said that unlike Pythagoras, regular people had to develop certain skills in order to hear this "music". According to Pythagoras, when the planets rotated, their friction against each other produced sounds that created musical compositions. He called these compositions " the harmony of the spheres," and "the song of planets." He said that human ears could not hear this unique music, just like a man living by the sea could not hear the sound of waves, yet the soul of every man reacted to this harmony and lived according to this universal symphony. The poetry of Pythagoras' beliefs inspired generations of scientists. Astronomer Johannes Kepler developed the ideas of Pythagoras in his book, *The Harmony of the World*. The idea of the "music of the spheres" was echoed in the 20th century in atomic physics, when the same harmony was discovered in the microscopic atom.

> **"Appearance makes a statue beautiful, actions make man beautiful."**

Today it seems difficult to believe that Pythagoras' ideas about the mathematical basis of the universe were made 25 centuries ago, at the very beginning of scientific research. His ideas were not scientifically proven then, but today they are accepted by modern researchers.

The scale of Pythagoras' personality is amazing. How could one man unite the knowledge of such different nations? It required a tremendous spirit and a strong intellect to become the leader of a city, to create a "Republic of Scientists," and to develop a new world vision for human kind.

The Pythagorean Unions, founded 2,500 year ago, laid the foundations of modern mathematics, philosophy, and universal science. The ideas of Pythagoras established for future generations a confidence in the human mind, and resulted in a number of discoveries, which were offered to the world by the greatest minds of Ancient Greece.

Pythagoras' teachings about universal harmony inspired many thinkers, including Copernicus, Johannes Kepler, Leonardo da Vinci, Newton, Albert Einstein, and many other scientists who shared his belief in the relevance, the beauty, and the harmony of a nature built on mathematical principles.

Pythagoras was and will remain the master of thoughts, and the very incarnation of the ideals he defended.

CONFUCIUS
(551-479 BC)

An Ancient Chinese thinker, and the founder of Confucianism. Generations of inhabitants in the Middle Kingdom regard him as the Father of the Nation, and the Master of Life. For a majority of people in Southeast Asia today, the teachings of Confucianism remain an important part of their daily thoughts, efforts, and actions.

"To learn without thinking is a useless effort."

In the rich imagination of storytellers, real historical happenings can become fantastic events, and the factual lives of famous historical figures can become mixed with legend.. However, Chinese historians documented Confucius' actions during his life without exaggeration. Only his conception and birth were described using bright, fantastic words. One cannot blame historians for their exaggeration on this event; Confucius was born during a very difficult period of Chinese history.

It was during times of defeat for China, formerly a great power, that Confucius was born. The Great Chinese Empire had broken like a jar into many small feuding kingdoms, none of which recognized the Emperor as their supreme ruler. Several centuries of internal fighting had finally destroyed the country. The people lived in abject poverty as a result of constant civil war. Farmers had to put all of their efforts into war construction, so their fields were neglected. Laws did not apply anymore, religion lost its role, and cultural values inherited from the wise emperors of the past were being slowly forgotten; people were going backward. The people of China had lost their way to heaven, the Tao, and the country urgently needed structural changes. It needed new civic and criminal laws, measures to improve living standards, and new ethical codes to improve everyday life.

This great task was undertaken by a modest civil servant of aristocratic descent, who would come to be known as Confucius. According to historical documents, the genealogy of the great thinker goes back to Emperor Huang Di, who ruled the Empire in 2,637 years BC, and who entered history as the inventor of the compass. Other of Confucius' ancestors became famous as outstanding civil and military leaders. His father, Shu Liang, dedicated his entire life to military service, and became famous for his unusual strength and bravery. After he ended his military career, he was put in charge of a small town in the kingdom of Lu. From his first marriage he had no male descendant, so at the age of 70 he married the young Qing Qi, who soon gave him a son.

According to historical documents, signs and miracles accompanied the very conception, pregnancy, and birth of Confucius. His young mother selected the place to give birth - a tree on a hill - according to instructions from the sky. On the night Confucius was born, two dragons were blowing on the hill, and unicorns were guarding the tree. The air was full of harmonious sounds. A spring of pristine, warm water came out of the ground and disappeared after the baby had been washed. The historical documents mention that the baby had a very unusual look: "his mouth was like a lake, his lips were like those of a buffalo, and he had the back of a dragon." According to chronological tables, Confucius was born in 551 BC. When he was born, he was given the name of Qiu (which means Hill) in memory of the hill where his mother prayed to God to send her a son. Years later, Qui's followers started calling him Confucius, which literally means "Master King".

At the age of three Confucius lost his father, and his very young mother took charge of his education. He behaved very well, outsmarted children of his age, gave respect to older people, and soon developed a keen interest in the traditions of his country. He preferred ceremonies to children's games.

At the age of seven Confucius entered a boarding school. Even at that time in China there were schools in the villages. The ancient leaders of China knew that only education could save the nation, so primary school became compulsory, regardless of birth. Education started with basic manners. Only once they had mastered this important subject could children carry on with the study of rituals, and later the study of archery. The most talented children, regardless again of their birth, were accepted at the age of 15 into high schools, where they were taught ethical philosophy. Confucius was such a successful student that at the age of 17 he became assistant to his master, the famous scholar Ping Chung, and worked as a tutor. Very wise for his age, Confucius tried not to make his friends envious, and encouraged them to follow his example. During those years of self-education Confucius managed to obtain the fundamental knowledge that later impressed his followers.

> **"A man of dignity must be educated and must have a strong will. His burden is heavy, and his road is long."**

After high school Confucius became a civil servant, as his mother wished. His duties were small, but came with much responsibility. Confucius was responsible for the quality of the stock in the shops and markets. In the early morning hours the 18 year-old inspector patrolled the food markets with his assistants, and carefully verified all of the products. He praised honest merchants and severely punished those breaking the law. In his free time he studied science as before, but he also met with farmers, asking them about the different types of soil, and the different methods for improving soil fertility. He wanted to gain knowledge about his profession. When he worked at the grain markets, which were state stocked in case of bad harvest, he became an expert in long-term grain conservation. In other words, he studied every matter related, even remotely, to his duty. As a result he was very successful professionally, and he was promoted to a position of greater responsibility. He became inspector of arable fields, forests and cattle, and King Lu gave him the right to change old rules and introduce new regulations. In this position, the young, talented official introduced progressive changes. According to historical documents, thanks to his efforts, "sterile fields became fertile again; the cattle improved and became numerous."

At the age of 19 Confucius married Qi Guan Shi, a girl of a well known family. A year later, their son was born. In order to celebrate this event, King Lu sent a pair of carps as a gift to the young couple. The grateful father gave the name of Li to the baby, as Li means carp in Chinese, and added Bo You (the eldest of brothers). Despite this hopeful name, Confucius's next child was a daughter, and he had no more sons.

From his high position, Confucius could see the problems affecting the state. Noticing the lack of dedication in young civil servants, and the misery of the people, the young thinker realized that his country was in trouble. He turned to the texts of the ancient kingdoms, and found that his own thoughts were confirmed by his readings. The legal and moral foundations that were the basis of the Middle Kingdom, were no longer relevant.

Because the ancient leaders of China were convinced that the earth and the sky were secretly connected, they considered the harmony of society (the earth) essential to maintaining their rule (the sky), and they tried to improve the morals of their people by their own good example. They were themselves considered to be Heaven's Sons, holy and unapproachable, but they knew that their positions were guaranteed only as long as they protected the wealth of the people. If they didn't, Heaven gave the people the right to protest. "Heaven's view can be seen in the view of the people; what does not please Heaven can be seen in the people's will," stated the old holy books that Confucius read. "The Master is the vessel, and the people are the water. The shape of the vessel shapes the water." With these simple words, the wise men of the past expressed the burden of responsibility put on the shoulders of the Son of Heaven. The ancient book's description of the first Chinese emperors, known as Emperor-Benefactors, showed that the Emperor was considered the father of the nation only if he was concerned with the nine benefits: "water, fire, metal, wood, bread, sustainable use, harmonious living with others, good health, and the protection of life."

Confucius realized that Heaven was not pleased, and he became convinced that the only way to save China was to return to the ethical values inherited from the past.

"A man of dignity does not follow other people."

Confucius' success in civil service soon made him famous in the kingdom of Lu. Such a start meant a brilliant career in administration, but the sudden death of his mother, who had just turned 34, forced him to leave his career. Old traditions required that a son should follow a three-year mourning after the death of his parents. In those days, many civil servants ignored traditions and did not follow that rule, but Confucius respected old rules, loved his mother immensely, and could not ignore his duties as a son.

The general moral and cultural decay of the period affected even funereal traditions. Confucius' contemporaries ignored ancient customs, and buried their relatives without ritual, showing little respect to the dead. While preparing for his mother's funeral, Confucius took on the role of a civic master.

He said, "Each of us is just a link in the chain of human race. We owe everything to our ancestors. Without them, we would not be here. While alive, they gave us protection, and we must repay them by following the old rituals, established centuries ago. Honor, given to those who were here before us, will be repaid to us by our descendants."

Confucius' opinions were heard by his contemporaries, and nearly forgotten traditions were given new life.

During the three-year mourning period Confucius lived alone, as tradition required. Having abandoned his duties, the young philosopher was able to dedicate himself to self-education. The pain caused by the loss of his mother did not go away, but studying kept him busy. Confucius hoped that in his readings he would find answers to difficult questions: How could he rescue his country from chaos? How could he breathe life into a once grand state, now destroyed, divided, and ruined?

"The one who can turn to the old and see the new, is worthy of becoming a master."

Confucius dedicated all of his time to the holy books and texts of the ancient kingdoms. He studied the rules of Huang Di, Yao, Shun, and the emperors of the Xia and Zhou dynasties, who ruled over a peaceful and prosperous China.

The lives of the Emperor-Benefactors became Confucius' models for moral living and effective state ideology. In his mind, he became very close to the almost mythical figures. Later, when developing his ideas about ethics and the structure of the state in Chinese society, he attributed his ideas to the great emperors of past centuries.

He could not have done it any other way. China was in a deep crisis, and huge changes were needed to please Heaven. A complete ideological, cultural, and state revolution was necessary. As a man of wisdom, Confucius knew very well that to safeguard stability these radical changes had to look like they were merely a resurgence of the ideals of the past. So when explaining his new principles, the young philosopher quoted authorities recognized by every Chinese citizen.

When Confucius' mourning period came to an end he put his mourning clothes on his mother's grave, as was customary. Then he continued with his research instead of going back to his former position. The old books were a rich ground for Confucius' thoughts, and the philosopher became utterly convinced that the only way to revive China was to remember its past.

Confucius hadn't turned 30 yet, and already people were coming from all over China to seek his wisdom. Young and old, famous and simple, rich and poor, all came to him for answers to essential questions, and for advice in their lives. One day the King of Yen sent his assistant to ask Confucius how to rule the state.

Confucius responded, "Since I do not know your king, his subjects, or his country, I cannot give you any recommendations, but if your king were to ask me how the ancient kings would act in a certain situation, I could easily give a full answer. I only speak of what I know."

In response to Confucius' words, the king of Yen invited him to the palace to serve him. Confucius was asked to work out a plan for law reform, and the improvement of morals. A year later, after he successfully accomplished his task, Confucius left the palace of King Yen. He was convinced that he could be useful in his efforts to restore his crumbling country, and inspired by his success in Yen, he continued with his research.

Confucius returned to his home kingdom of Lu, and despite the efforts of his relatives to convince him to return to his former position, he turned down a career as a civil servant. "My task is to serve and be useful to people," he said. "The country is now in darkness, and people need support. Our Heaven is a victim of internal fighting, but I know we are all one family, and my mission is to protect the family."

By then his house had turned into an academy with a growing number of students. Some of these students became his devoted followers, and remained close to him throughout his life. They noted down all the words of the sage and made drawings of his face. These notes later made Lun Yu famous when he wrote *The Book of Conversations and Discourses,* a masterpiece of Confucianism.

Many aphorisms of the famous Chinese sage are used in the everyday lives of people with very different cultures and beliefs. These aphorisms have gained their own independent life, and when quoting them, one often forgets to mention the name of their author:

"Do not do to others what you do not wish for yourself."

"If you have no evil thoughts, you will do no evil actions."

"Happy is the one who is ignorant, for he is at no risk of being misunderstood."

"Do not complain that your neighbor's roof is covered with snow, when your threshold is not clean."

Confucius was convinced that with a little effort from every person in the Middle Kingdom, the Golden Age of the Empire could be returned. To ensure success, every human being had to expect the best of himself/herself, and respect the common moral rules and laws. Confucius' loyal students took notes of the philosopher's thoughts on these common moral rules and laws, in order to keep a record of them for future generations:

"If one rules through laws, and keeps order through punishment, people will try to avoid punishment, and will experience no shame. If one rules through good actions, and keeps order through rituals, people will feel ashamed and will improve..."

"If you rule the people with dignity, they will be respectful. If you treat the people well, they will work diligently. If you give praise to the wise, and discipline to the ignorant, the people will trust you..."

"You can force the people to obey, but you cannot force them to understand why."

Confucius started his career as a political thinker and a master of state wisdom, but he soon switched his focus to the ideology of peace.

The Kingdom under Heaven was turning to ruins and desolation, while Confucius was in the Kingdom of Lu, focused on finding the ideal harmony between the state and the person. He knew that not all of his requirements could be met, but he also knew that society needed more than just down-to-earth programs of change. Ideals were essential to sustaining the ethics and the spirit of a nation.

"When acknowledging routine matters, a gentleman does not reject or approve, but measures everything with justice."

The young ruler of the kingdom of Qi invited Confucius to his palace, telling the philosopher that he could use his advice and methods. When Confucius entered the palace with his students, he was greeted with full honors. However, he was soon disappointed to find that the young king spent his time in leisure and pleasure, and only invited Confucius to boost his own fame. The young man was flattered that a real philosopher was sitting next to him, and was interested in having a conversation with an educated man, but he became bored when Confucius tried to talk about state matters. The ruler was not willing to study, so life gave its own lesson.

One day a conversation between the king and the philosopher was interrupted. A messenger arrived to inform them that lightning had destroyed a temple dedicated to the ancestors in the imperial palace of the kingdom of Zhou. For the Chinese of this period, a fire in a temple was more than an accident; it was a sign from above, and a sort of warning. Shortly after the messenger left, the pair resumed their conversation.

"The fire took place in the temple of Li Wang, is that true, my king?" asked Confucius.

"Why do you think it took place in that specific temple?" asked the king.

"Sooner or later, heaven punishes the ones who break the rules," answered the sage.

Li Wang was a real tyrant. He had eliminated the wise regulations of his ancestors, and introduced luxury into the palace, destroying his country for his own wealth. Confucius believed that his celestial punishment was the destruction of the temple constructed in his memory, as he did not deserve such respect. It was also a warning to other kings not to follow the example of Li Wang.

The king was troubled by the words of the philosopher. He sent a messenger to find out which temple had been destroyed by lightning, and when a few days later the messenger confirmed that it was Li Wang's temple that had burned, the young king could not hide his astonishment from the philosopher.

"Confucius, you are the greatest man of the Empire!" exclaimed the king enthusiastically. With his Inner Eye, a learned man can not only see the present and the past, but also what ordinary people do not see. The enthusiastic young ruler wanted to offer Confucius the whole city, but the philosopher refused. When Confucius had accepted the invitation, he had done so with the thought that he would be useful in bringing about change for the inhabitants of Qi, but instead he had spent a year listening to an egotistical, irresponsible ruler.

An admirer of Confucius, a rich and influential dignitary, died in Confucius' home kingdom of Lu, and before his death he instructed his sons to study the rules of Li - ritual ceremonies - with Confucius. After their mourning period was over, the sons asked the philosopher to accept them as students. They had money and influence, which greatly helped Confucius' situation, and they decided to help Confucius accomplish his dream: to visit the capital of the empire, where he could become familiar with the ceremonies and rules of the Zhou Dynasty.

The capital made a tremendous impression on Confucius, who admired the ancient temples and frescoes, but the greatest impression was left by seeing the moral sayings of the ancient sages in a gold engraving. Reading the thousand year-old Chinese characters, the philosopher told his students, "Those sayings are all the wisdom that can be learned in a human life. Study them, for by following those rules, we can reach perfection."

When Confucius was introduced to the First Minister of the kingdom of Zhou, the minister asked him about his teachings. The philosopher gave the following answer, as usual:

"These teachings, which are called mine, go back in fact to the emperors Yao and Shun. My method of teaching is simple. I point to the experience of the ancient sages as a model, and I recommend that people read the ancient books, and adapt their advice to our current situation."

"Yet, how can we gain wisdom?" asked the Minister, "give us some advice."

The philosopher thought for a second, and then said:

"Here are four rules that can be of use to you. Remember that iron breaks, no matter how strong it is, what looks indestructible is often easy to break down, a proud man thinks he is watched and worshipped, when he is really scorned and ignored, a man who is too condescending, and humors others to reach his goals, becomes the victim of his own behavior." These rules might seem simple at first glance, but for those who fully understand and follow them, they are full of wisdom.

Interaction between the state and the people was an essential part of the teachings of Confucius. According to him, the main rule one should follow in order to be a sound ruler, is to take the middle way.

When Confucius was shown to the throne room, he directed the attention of the mandarins (high - ranking Chinese officials) to the bucket of stone, next to the throne.

"Why is this bucket next to the throne?" asked the philosopher.

They were not able to give him a clear answer, so Confucius asked one of the mandarins to get water from the well with the bucket. The bucket would not dip into the water, but instead floated on the surface.

"Obviously, we must do this in a different way," suggested the philosopher, and asked another mandarin to try. The second mandarin threw the bucket into the well with all his strength, and the bucket filled with water and sunk to the bottom of the well. It was too heavy to be lifted out, unless the water was spilled out of it.

"I guess I will have to try myself," said Confucius, dubiously. He took the bucket, and after carefully balancing it, dropped it into the well. Carefully, and slowly, he filled it with water to the rim, and brought it up.

"This is an example of the Golden Rule - to follow the middle way. Extreme softness is as inappropriate as extreme severity. In ancient times, when a new Emperor was to get on the throne, this experiment was part of the coronation. The law required that this bucket be kept next to the throne, so that the Emperor would always remember the lesson taught by this simple physical experiment."

By asking questions, and sometimes answering them, Confucius was able to teach his students the basics of his philosophy. His message was that high ethical standards, mixed with humanistic policies, was the key to a healthy, prosperous state. A state could only exist with the full trust of the people.

Confucius was able to teach his countless students the basics of ethics by using simple examples from life. According to the student's notes, they were once enjoying a walk around the city when Confucius approached a bird merchant. He pointed out to his students that only young birds were in the cages.

"You only sell young birds?" Confucius asked the bird merchant.

"No, it's just that it is hard to catch older birds. They are careful and do not trust anyone. They do not approach a trap until they have well studied the surroundings, and they warn younger birds as soon as they suspect danger. Only young, inexperienced birds fall into the trap, and if older birds are with them, only the ones following the younger birds fall into the trap."

"Did you hear these words?" asked the teacher. "Did you catch the deep meaning of what was said? Isn't that true for humans too? Lack of awareness and self-confidence causes suffering in young people. If they don't listen to the advice of elders and the educated, they will often fall into traps. However, older people can sometimes become taken with the excitement of younger people, and follow them into the same traps. Remember, young people will avoid misfortune when the wisdom of older people keeps them back. Old people find misfortune when they are seduced by the enthusiasm of the younger. Remember the words of this bird merchant, and use them in your life!"

> **"To overcome ones selfish nature and return to ones duties is to have a sense of humanity. Whether we are to be human or not, is all up to us."**

The sage spent two years in the capital city. Upon his return to the kingdom of Lu he found desolation and destruction. A few influential families had overthrown the king and taken over. Too concerned with their own daily lives, the families neglected their country, and did not seek Confucius' help.

According to the notes of his loyal students, the teacher spent 15 years in the kingdom of Lu. During those years he slept for only 2 hours per day, and continued with his research in the ancient books, considered holy by every inhabitant of the Middle Kingdom. He edited the great works of the past, focusing on the most relevant ideas, explaining obscure parts, and reducing the parts that were no longer relevant. The result of those years of effort was the *Shu Jing (Book of History)*, which described the history of Ancient China as written by the historians of Huang Di. The original work depicted events in history, beginning with the year 2,365 BC. Confucius reduced the number of chapters to 50, and started the chronology of Chinese Emperors at Emperor Yao, before summarizing each period.

During his fifteen years in Lu, Confucius also wrote his historical work, *Chun Qiu (Spring and Autumn)*, focusing on the history of the Zhou dynasty. After finishing this huge work, he edited a book on old verses and songs, called the *Shi Jing (Book of Songs)*. Confucius reduced the number of songs from 3,000 to 311, keeping only the best. He remembered those songs by heart, and loved to sing them for his students. During his stay in the kingdom of Zhou, the teacher wrote a book on music. He considered music to be not only the highest form of art, but also the highest form of ruling, because he believed that music could feed the spirit of the people, and teach moral and human qualities.

Unable to cope with the misery of his home state any longer, Confucius decided to journey across China, but he found that the rest of China was miserable as well. Images of destruction, poverty and moral decay followed him almost everywhere he went. Only in the surroundings of the Tian Shan mountains did the patriarchal purity of the life of local farmers bring hope to his heart.

Confucius' journey took him though the kingdom of Qi once again. Twenty years had passed since his first visit there. The King of Qi was no longer a boy, but a mature, experienced ruler. Followed by his attendants, he received Confucius with full honor, and asked the teacher to enter the palace first.

"You are the greatest Son of Heaven, and my teacher," he said. "For me, a man of wisdom stands higher than a king. May I persuade you to accept this honor from the kingdom of Qi!"

Confucius refused to enter the room first, because he knew that it was against the customs and rituals. "Lord," he responded, "the etiquette is the same for all of us. Neither you, nor I can neglect our duties, and we should not amend the way things have always been done. Nobody should refuse the honors that are due to you, considering your rank. The state can prosper only when each person knows his or her position and duties. The ruler must be the ruler, the subject must be the subject, the father must be the father, and the son must be the son."

The king needed a wise adviser, and expressed his wish to name Confucius his First Minister. However, he was convinced by his jealous assistants to give up the idea. The sage was disappointed with the ruler once again. He had appeared to be a mature and responsible man, but it turned out that he was very weak, and dependant on his assistants.

When the teacher returned home to Lu, things were even worse. There was a bad harvest, and the people were extremely poor. They could not pay taxes. In this extreme situation, the authorities remembered Confucius. There were still some people in the kingdom of Lu who remembered that Confucius had worked effectively as a civil servant, and that under his rule even the most desolated lands gave good harvest.

The First Minister invited the sage to the palace, and asked for advice on how to bring an end to the terrible situation, but Confucius gave no answer.

"Why do you refuse to share your experience with us?" asked his students in astonishment. "Is the fate of your country irrelevant to you?"

Confucius explained, "The Minister is only concerned with raising more taxes, and all he wants to learn from me is how to improve his revenues from agriculture. I will not help this man, who is only interested in making money by taking even more advantage of our miserable people".

In the mean time, the situation only became worse. There

was no food in the kingdom of Lu, and the farmers were starving. In those difficult days, a leader from the palace offered one thousand measures of rice to Confucius to express his respect, hoping to gain friendship with the sage. Confucius accepted the present, but to the leader's surprise, did not express his thanks. This behavior surprised the students even more than the leader, but soon they understood. Confucius distributed all the rice to poor people, and in doing so he taught a lesson to the poor, to his students, and to the leader.

"He expected me to thank him, but instead hundreds of people thanked him. I hope that now he will understand how to distribute his riches. I acted as I was supposed to. I did not offend the leader by refusing his gift, but instead of selfishly keeping it all for myself, I distributed it to the people who really needed it."

When a few years later the legal king returned to the kingdom of Lu, he offered Confucius a high position in which he would be in charge of the residences and fortresses. In his new position, Confucius carefully studied the current system of agriculture, classifying different kinds of earth, and introducing alternative uses of the earth. He used the experiences of the ancient emperors as much as he could, and at the same time he introduced innovations, in an effort to make the best use of the most fertile ground.

Gradually, little by little, the situation of the people started improving, and with the improvement of their economic situation, their morale grew stronger. The king had a growing trust in his talented administrator. He proposed that Confucius become the Supreme Judge in the kingdom of Lu, and asked the sage to review old laws, and if necessary, prepare new laws relevant to the period.

When Confucius turned fifty, he became second in the

state, and could at last use his resources to serve society.

> **"When the state is ruled by common sense, poverty and needs disappear. When the state is ruled by nonsense, wealth and honor disappear."**

While serving in his new position, Confucius remained loyal to himself, and did not neglect his principles. He praised the worthy, and severely punished criminals, regardless of their position. Confucius' nature made him opposed to extreme measures, but nonetheless, he made the death penalty the required punishment for any high ranking official who had abused his power in order to earn money. Confucius enforced this law in a number of corruption cases.

When Confucius' students asked him for one word that should rule people's lives, they received the following answer: "compassion".

After learning of Confucius' enforcement of the death penalty, one student asked, "Didn't you teach us about compassion, Master? How can we understand your decision after such words?"

"If it was about the guilt of simple people, there would be no need to impose such a severe punishment," responded the sage. "Usually simple people who break the law are only half-guilty, or not even guilty at all, as they do not know their duties. Therefore compassion must be used. But criminals of high ranks, especially civil servants, are an example for the people, and therefore must be severely punished. The ancient books say that the 'death penalty applies in cases of big crimes committed on purpose.' The responsibility of statesmen is to educate the people and teach them the five basic duties: love for one another, and love for truth, loyalty, honor and justice. People must be taught justice, and must be punished only when they break the law on purpose!"

For Confucius, state policy was meant to educate people, and he never forgot this priority.

Once an old man came to Confucius with his son, and complained about how his son had been misbehaving. As the High Judge, Confucius made the decision to give them both a three-month a jail sentence. When he asked the pair back at the end of the three months, he asked the father the reason for his son's misbehavior. The father acknowledged that he was himself responsible for his son's actions, as he had failed to manage his son's wrath. Confucius praised him for his honesty and added:

"To educate a son is the first duty of a father, and this responsibility should not be passed over to courts. Do not lose hope. The only real mistake is in failing to correct your past mistakes."

To the young man the sage said, "Remember that your holiest duty is to obey your parents. You must respect them and take care of them. A respectful son can only disappoint his parents when he falls sick!"

Eventually Confucius was able to bring back the people's trust in their laws and government. The king highly appreciated Confucius' skills, and since Confucius knew about the human soul, he often asked him for advice. Soon the kingdom of Lu became a powerful state, and its neighbors looked at it as a potentially dangerous force.

The neighboring states began trying to undermine Confucius' influence on the government. Their intentions were compatible with the wishes of a number of civil servants in the kingdom of Lu, who had lost their weight and influence because of Confucius' new rules. Controversy began to poison

Confucius' life. At the same time, the king was being overwhelmed with gifts and presents from his neighbors, yesterday's enemies. He became more and more involved in entertainment, neglecting matters of state. Once, in the middle of festivities, Confucius was bold enough to remind the king of his duties. The king was strongly irritated, indicating that Confucius' advise was no longer desired.

Once again, Confucius took to the road with his devoted students. He brought his teachings everywhere he went, trying to influence the state by attracting the attention of influential people. Rulers greeted him with great respect, but he was not successful in his efforts to convince them to bring about change. They didn't understand the need for change, and were used to solving state problems with weapons.

"It is impossible to find a common language because we have diverging principles," the sage used to say. He experienced the truth of these words in the last years of his life.

"Having discovered the truth in the morning, one can die in the evening."

In those days the number of Confucius' students had reached 3,000, and crowds of people were coming from all over to hear the great sage speak. Not all rulers were happy with Confucius' popularity. Some considered Confucius a troublemaker, and were eager to get rid him. In the kingdom of Song, the philosopher and his students established their camp in a clearing with a huge, luxurious tree in the middle. In the shadow of these branches, Confucius held conversations with his students about religion, morals, traditions and rituals that had been inherited from their ancestors, and discussed with them how social harmony depended on the efforts of every inhabitant of the Middle Kingdom. The local population came to the clearing to hear the teachings of the sage.

"After meeting a man of honor," said Confucius, "think of how you compare to him. After meeting a man of low morals, look inside and judge yourself." The teacher continued, "Remember that 5 elements contribute to the perfect gentleman: seriousness, honesty, a strong will, goodness and a generous soul."

"Teacher, you mentioned the soul. Does eternity exist?" asked one of the listeners.

"If we do not know about life, how can we know about death?" answered the philosopher, ironically.

In the mean time, the military leader of the kingdom of Song decided to expel Confucius from the kingdom. He ordered that the tree be cut down, and chased away Confucius' supporters, but this was not the most dramatic incident in the life of Confucius. In the kingdom of Cai, the local officials threw Confucius and his students in prison, fearing their influence on the state. For a whole week the teacher had to endure prison life, and at the same time maintain high spirits for his students. When the doors of their cell finally opened, Confucius and his students fled the city.

When Confucius turned 70, the life of a wanderer did not seem appropriate any longer, but he still had a challenging plan ahead of him. He wanted to go on a pilgrimage to the Holy Tian Shan Mountains. In ancient times, human sacrifice took place on the highest peaks of these mountains, and the teacher wanted to reach the altar of his ancestors at the end of his life.

On the first mountain leading to the holy place, Confucius noticed a woman praying over a fresh grave. He approached her to express his condolences, and learned that within one year her whole family, from her mother-in-law to her husband

and son, had been killed by a tiger.

"Why did you not leave this place?" asked Confucius, in shock from her story.

"There are no cruel rulers here," answered the woman in tears.

"Did you hear the words of this poor woman?" asked the philosopher of his students. "Remember, a cruel ruler is worse than a tiger."

From the top of the Holy Mountain, Confucius looked at the view. It looked as if the Middle Kingdom had opened its arms to him, but the view of abandoned temples brought sadness to the heart of Confucius. The heritage of the ancient wise men, and the laws of ethics, were forgotten. All of his efforts to renew national and state identity were useless. Not a single leader agreed to implement his ideas, and his efforts to make people more human and kindhearted were vain. A deadly sadness fell upon Confucius' life.

"My days are numbered," said the sage to his devoted students, "I give you my books. In these I have compiled the precious heritage of the ancients - all the necessary knowledge and rules of wisdom. Please keep these books pure and pass them on to your descendants; maybe they can appreciate their value! Do not hope that during these times of ignorance, you can propagate these ideas. As you can see, I was not very successful myself! "

Confucius paid respect to the altar of the ancestors, and returned to the kingdom of Lu with his followers. He had given up hope of being heard by any king. All that remained was to dedicate his last days to lessons with his students. He wanted to raise support for a more human way of ruling by educating "perfect gentlemen".

Three hundred loyal followers built a village in the hills. In a small gazebo under an apricot tree, the thinker worked on his historical texts, and the final edit of his Canons. Confucius' circle of followers became his second family. He was open in his conversation with them because they shared his views.

Confucius discussed with them his sacred mission to create perfect gentlemen who would conquer the world according to their ideals. He explained that the most important quality of a perfect man is his Ren - his sense of love for human kind. This refers not only to his love for his friends, but also his love for his state and its subjects. When one student asked Confucius to be more specific about the idea of love for human kind, the sage responded, "A man who loves human kind must embody 5 elements, dignity, generosity, justice, quickness, and a kind heart. Dignity avoids humiliation, generosity wins all over, justice brings trust, quickness allows success, and a kind heart allows for commanding people."

Confucius said that a perfect gentleman must have the quality of Wen - a curiosity, along with an interest in education, spirituality, and self-improvement. Confucius believed that an educated man was a better man, and that studies should not stop at a young age because they were necessary to the development of a personality.

The philosopher believed that you could judge people by the way they regarded education. "The ones who have intuitive knowledge stand above others," he said. "They are followed by the ones who earn knowledge through studies. Then come the ones experiencing problems in their studies. The ones who have a hard time studying and do not study, stand even lower," explained the great Chinese pedagogue to his spiritual children. He also liked to say that a man with deep knowledge could enter a new dimension. He could broaden his outlook by broadening his inner world.

Besides the Ren and the Wen, the Li - the knowledge of etiquette and moral rules - was a quality that differentiated a perfect gentleman from an ordinary person. Confucius believed that without Li there could be no harmonic relationships among people, and that in all life situations a gentleman must strictly follow the Li. According to Confucius, the most important rule of the Li was to "respect every man, as you would yourself, and act toward others as you wish others would act toward you." The teacher explained, "There is nothing above this."

In the shadow of apricot trees, surrounded by his students, the wise old man described ideals that all perfect gentlemen should strive for in all situations. These ideal were a human heart, and the balance and harmony that comes from following the middle path. Only gentlemen embodying the strength of the Ren, Wen, and Li, could rule appropriately. Confucius' perfect gentlemen were supposed to accomplish what the sage could not accomplish. They were supposed to create a new social order, and return to China the Tao - the Way to Heaven.

"Each of us can become a gentleman. We only need to decide to do so," repeated the philosopher, whose strength was diminishing every day. He felt that he was becoming weaker, and put all of his soul into these words.

When the sage died, his students buried him with full honor. They built three hills around his grave, and the king of Lu ordered the construction of a chapel to house the works of Confucius on an altar.

Despite Confucius' fears, his teachings were not lost. His presence and teachings only grew during the centuries. A hundred years after Confucius' death, a chapel was built in every Chinese city to honor him. Two centuries after his death, Confucius was declared a saint, and people went on pilgrimages to his grave. During the two centuries of the Han dynasty, his work, the *Lun Yu*, became part of the classic canon, and later, during the Tang dynasty, his texts were engraved in stone and declared state relics. Starting from this period, the teachings of the philosopher became an essential part of state ideology and culture. The Chinese bureaucracy made its own interpretation of Confucianism, and used it for guidance.

Even in their bureaucratic interpretation, the teachings of Confucius remained human. The sage of Lu expressed the spirit of the people, so his teachings remained within the people and survived all political changes and disasters. Confucianism came to define the Chinese way of thinking, and the national characteristics of the Chinese nation. They became an essential element of the Chinese soul. For more than 2,000 years, the Chinese people have kept Confucianism as their reference for living. For them, Confucius remains the perfect sage, the father of the nation, and the master of ten thousand generations.

Confucianism is still part of spiritual life in today's China, as well as a number of South-Asian countries. It has become the spiritual reference for the most populated part of the world. The children of Japan, Korea, and Vietnam all memorize the first sentence of the legendary Lun Yu. That sentence reads:

"To learn and practice what has been used throughout history is a pleasure, is it not? To have friends come from afar to see you is joyful, is it not? To be unperturbed when unappreciated by others is gentlemanly, is it not?"

Perhaps the surprising economic success of East Asia has its root in the teachings of Confucius. The joy of learning, combined with work, and the desire for new things, combined with self-improvement - isn't this the secret of the Asian Miracle?

In 1979 Deng Xiaoping announced his program aimed at modernizing the Chinese economy, and stated that his goal was to reach, by the year 2000, the prosperity of the Xiao Kan society. According to historians, Xiao Kan aimed for average development, and the general improvement of society. Deng Xiaping's reference to Xiao Kan did not mean much to politicians or sinologists, but for Chinese intellectuals and Confucianists it referred to a saying of the wise teacher, Confucius. Using the Xia Kan society as a reference meant aiming for the ideal of a "society of moderate prosperity," as described by Confucius. This was not just an inspiring idea, but a plan that would help all of the inhabitants of the Middle Kingdom.

Now the modern civilized world watches the Chinese phenomenon with great attention, trying to decipher the secret of its success. The world wants to know how the citizens of China were able to accomplish Confucius' plan in only 20 years.

According to traditional Western philosophy dating back to the 17th century Renaissance, science is meant to adapt nature to the needs of human beings. The progress of science should solve all material and social problems, which should result in a period of order and good on earth. For this reason, technology and scientific potential have become the traditional criteria for the development of a civilized society.

People of the west call themselves the masters of the world. They are not concerned with tomorrow, and they abuse Mother Nature, requiring more and more sacrifices from her, all for the sake of their comfortable lives. Only in these last decades have they started to think seriously about the price imposed on their environment by their egocentrism.

The eternal Confucian teachings bring new meaning to today's environmental debate. His teachings stress that the environment is perfect and harmonious, until man and society destroy this harmony. Therefore, helping western society find harmony, will restore harmony to the environment, and therefore improve the quality of life for all of human kind.

Confucius' teachings are still relevant today, because for

25 centuries Chinese thinkers have judged society and individuals according to their influence on social and world harmony. I believe that all of us on this planet, regardless of our roles, need to appreciate the harmony that our actions can create. We should all remember the thoughts of Confucius, the great teacher of the ancient kingdom of Lu.

ARCHIMEDES
(Circa 287-212 BC)

The ancient Greek scientist Archimedes was blessed with many extraordinary talents. As an outstanding mathematician, astronomer, and engineer, he certainly belongs to a cohort of the greatest geniuses ever known to human kind.

The Innovator From Syracuse

For us, living at the end of the 20th century, science and engineering are forever connected to the concept of "scientific and technical progress." Today it seems hard to believe that for centuries, science maintained an arrogant distance from engineering. The grandiose constructions of the ancient past - the irrigation systems of Egypt, the palaces and stadiums of Greece, the roads and aqueducts of Rome - were constructed without the involvement of scientists. Science was described as a "payed slave labor." Archimedes' brilliant and unique talent, in contrast to the traditions of his time, fostered the union of science and engineering. He viewed them as complementary, rather than opposite, and demonstrated their consolidated power.

Archimedes was born in the city of Syracuse in Sicily, a Greek colony at the time. His father, Phidias, was a close relative of Hieron, the King of Syracuse, and he had gained a reputation as a good mathematician and astronomer, and a passionate admirer of the arts.

Since his early childhood, Archimedes was living in harmony with the world of numbers. He was fascinated with the precise beauty of their eternal rules. Mathematics became his passion. He showed disdain for daily chores, and devoted all of his time to his favorite occupation, sometimes forgetting about food and rest.

Archimedes received his education in Alexandria, the capital of Egypt, then ruled by Ptolemes. During that period, Alexandria was the center of Hellenic science and culture. It was famous for its ancient library, which contained 500,000 scrolls of papyrus. It was also the city that established the first museum, the Alexandrian. The cultural and scientific elite, including prominent poets, artists, musicians, sculptors, mathematicians, physicists, geometricians, and astronomers, all worked in that city.

In Alexandria, Archimedes became familiar with mainstream science and technical engineering, and, of course, studied the *Problems of Mechanics* by Aristotle with great care. The scientific community at that time was heavily influenced by the Aristotelian view on mechanics, which saw such an occupation as appropriate for slaves. The contemporaries of the young scientist shared the view that manual work was a disgrace for a free citizen, but still, it was mechanics that entirely absorbed the mind of the young Archimedes. He was led by his passion for discovery, and his enthusiasm as a researcher. He was eager to check his theoretical discoveries in practice. Most likely, that is the reason Archimedes wanted to return to his native city. In any case, it was Syracuse that became the birthplace of his great discoveries.

Leibnitz once said:
"After reading about Archimedes, one ceases to be astonished by the latest discoveries of mathematicians and engineers."

Archimedes laid the foundations for a new school of thought in the field of physics and mathematics, which later contributed greatly to an accelerated development of technical mechanics. Being equally sophisticated in scrupulous mathematical deliberations as in practical engineering, Archimedes astonished his contemporaries, as well as scientists of future generations. He managed to calculate the area of a circle and an ellipse, with great accuracy. He was also able to calculate the volume of an ellipsoid and a sphere, and the paraboloid of a revolution. He discovered the value of the relation between the circumference of a circle and its diameter, with tremendous accuracy, to be 3.14. It is noteworthy that a majority of his contemporaries were satisfied with the less accurate value of three.

Long before the emergence of the rules for extracting square roots, Archimedes extracted roots from very large numbers. In his discourses on mathematics he came close to the creation of an integral calculus, based on the fundamentals of mathematical analysis. These works proved to be ahead of their time, and they had a decisive impact on the development of mathematics in the 16th and 17th centuries. Archimedes' real successors emerged in the 17th century in the persons of Galileo and Newton.

Archimedes' discoveries in mechanics caused real breakthroughs. On the basis of a modest knowledge inherited from his predecessors, and a few principles that came to him intuitively, he made ingenious discoveries. Proceeding from a special case of symmetry, he created the theory of levers, and, understanding that the laws of levers were universal, he created a chain of theories and principles that provided the basis for mechanical statistics.

"Give me a place to stand, and I will move the earth."

This sentence, attributed to Archimedes, has become legendary. Having an extraordinary capability to solve technical puzzles with ease, Archimedes used his skills for practical purposes. Before the eyes of the ruler of Syracuse, and a crowd of astonished eyewitnesses, he pushed the largest three mast cargo ship of those times, called "The Syracuse," into the water by himself. It weighed 4,200 tons. This feat was possible because of a complex system of levers and polispasts. Interestingly, the inventor of polispasts, an elaborate freight shipment mechanism consisting of several blocks, is Archimedes himself.

The scientist's mind knew no rest. Once, while sitting in a full bath, he discovered that part of the water spilled over the bath onto the floor. Archimedes was struck with the idea that there was a displacement force that impacted objects submerged in liquid. Forgetting all else, he ran out into the streets of Syracuse without any clothes on, shouting "Eureka!" ("I have discovered!").

The name of Archimedes has been given to more than one discovery. The Archimedes screw found broad use in water drainage. For centuries it was used to drain water from wells, and irrigate fields. The great Leonardo da Vinci used the Archimedes' screw as a principal unit in his design of a helicopter in 1475. The Archimedes screw is still used, as well as the Archimedes' spiral, in some mechanisms used for instrument making.

When a Genius Becomes the Defender of His Own Country

Archimedes demonstrated his technical genius in the field of war. History has it that in 213 BC the Romans, under the leadership of Chief Consul Marcellus, laid siege on the Greek city of Syracuse by land and sea. The Romans had won many victories by that time and had no doubts about their strength, but the Greeks were able to face the challenge. Unwilling to comply with the will of the conquerors who were making every effort to establish their supremacy over the Mediterranean, the citizens of Syracuse agreed to delegate their most talented fellow countryman to supervise the defense of the city.

The Greek philosopher and moralist Plutarch wrote two centuries later that the Romans did not take into account the exceptional intellectual abilities of Archimedes. They had no idea that sometimes the genius of one person can do more than the accumulated power of several different people. For about two years Archimedes successfully defended the city from the invincible Roman army, with the help of his war machines. The technical machines created by Archimedes are still surprising to many.

Dozens of launchers built by Archimedes threw clouds of stones, spears, and darts, on the Romans. As the invaders approached the city there were at first long distance, and then short distance missile launchers put into action. Plutarch wrote, "It seemed as though no one could escape the strikes of Archimedes' launchers. Entire units fell down to the ground and the troops were taken with fear. At the same time as the ships were struck with heavy pointed sticks, some machines crashed them into the sea with a heavy blow, and others lifted them high in the sky, and then threw them back into the sea. Machines were launching the ships onto the rocks near the city walls, and their sailors were being subjected to a terrifying annihilation."

Based on this description of Archimedes' machines, don't they seem to anticipate robots?

Plutarch further wrote, "The losses were heavy and the panic on the ships was great. Archimedes positioned most of the machines inside the city walls, and it seemed to the Romans, attacked by the invisible missiles, that they were fighting with the gods. Archimedes alone was the soul of the whole defense system. He set everything in motion and managed the resistance. The Romans were so scared that one had only to show them a wooden stick or a rope, and they would run away shouting that Archimedes was pointing his machine on them".

Other sources report Archimedes' use of "solar lasers," or to be more precise, a system of mirrors that enabled the besieged townsmen to burn practically the entire Roman fleet. Sources indicate that when the Roman triremes (three mast ships) approached Syracuse from the sea, something incredible happened. They all started blazing up. The dazzling flames stupefied Marcellus' terrified soldiers. How did Archimedes manage to create a system of mirrors capable of reflecting the sunlight without diffusing it, in 200 BC? The dazzling light was thrown to the triremes by huge copper disks, but is it possible that it was flaming arrows that burned the ships, and not light reflected by the mirrors? Perhaps the mirrors had a different function. Perhaps they were used for taking an optical aim. Scientists still argue about this issue. The secret of the blazing tar also remains unsolved. The Syracuseans were hurling the Romans with huge shells and bombs made of a blazing tar mixture. According to legend, the tar even burned underneath the water's surface. This recipe is lost forever, along with the plans for Archimedes' war machines.

Roman historians couldn't conceal their admiration for the genius inventor. The experienced commander, Claudius Marcellus, was at a loss. He must have recognized the superiority of a scientist who could halt the Roman avalanche. However, in the end, Marcellus' soldiers managed to take the defenders of the city by surprise. At night, while the careless Syracuseans were celebrating the Artemis holiday, the Roman legions entered the city like a bloody storm, and spotted the genius Archimedes at work in the backyard of his house. He thought the noise and the cries in the streets were part of the celebrations.

"Soldier, stand away from my diagram," shouted the old man to the invaders, before the sword of a Roman legionnaire fell on his head. This was the final battle of a legendary inventor, an unsurpassed organizer of the defense of Syracuse, a genius mathematician, an engineer, an astronomer, and a man of unearthly talents. Undoubtedly, the Romans were hoping to take Archimedes' war inventions as their main trophy, but the farsighted scientist hadn't preserved a single sketch of the astonishing equipment. Plutarch wrote, "Archimedes had an elevated soul and a sophisticated mind, bearing tremendous knowledge in geometry. He did not want to leave a single book regarding the construction of those machines. That way the glory of the knowledge that exceeded human capabilities was his alone, and he was almost godly."

The famous Archimedes' sphere that decorated Syracuse became the only prize of the Romans, and was taken into the quarters of Marcellus, who was embittered by the series of shattering failures inflicted by the unyielding scientist. This creation, made by Archimedes himself from copper, was put in motion by a water engine, and was the first attempt to build a planetarium. It is known that one could observe the phases of the moon, the motion of the planets, and the sun and moon eclipses on this sphere. Archimedes was so proud of this invention that he devoted his only technical book to the sphere. It was called, *On how to make a Sphere*. Unfortunately, neither the book nor the legendary invention survived. Archimedes' grave was forgotten by his descendants, but it is known that the words the scientist wanted inscribed on his tomb were simply, "sphere" and "cylinder".

Many years after Archimedes' death, Marcus Tullius Cicero, who saw Archimedes' sphere in a Roman palace, wrote in his diary of his amazement at the scientist's genius. "The main miracle of Archimedes' creation was an imagination that combined different movements of various celestial bodies all in one system. One can see the sun replacing the moon in the same manner that it does everyday in the sky. One can see an eclipse, and the moon falling into the earth's shadow. The Sicilian was blessed with a rare talent and nature."

Archimedes was often referred to as Archimedes of Syracuse, but an individual like him belongs to our entire human civilization.

AVICENNA
(980 - 1037)

A prominent medieval scientist and encyclopedist, Avicenna lived in Central Asia and Iran, and served as a doctor and vizier to different rulers. Avicenna's scientific heritage can be traced through various fields. His medicine, philosophy, astronomy, mathematics, geology, botany, linguistics, music, and even poetry, profoundly influenced the development of natural sciences in the Middle Ages.

"A doctor has three weapons: words, plants, and a knife!"

Avicenna (Abu-Ali Ibn-Sina) is one of the greatest scientists and encyclopedists in the history of human kind. His scientific works have had a determining influence on the development of science and culture in the Muslim East, as well as in the Christian West.

Covering more than 1,500 pages with his immortal scientific work, Avicenna wrote discourse on various topics, and short articles that covered philosophy, medicine, astrology, mathematics, physics, chemistry, geography, music, logic and linguistics. The main part of his work consists of 40 volumes on medicine.

Avicenna's most important work is the five volume *Canon of Medicine*. This fundamental medical encyclopedia, written in Arabic, is an accumulation of the most advanced medicine in the known world at the end of the 11th century. It covers the extraordinarily rich knowledge held by doctors of Greek and Roman heritage, including Hippocrat and Galenus, and chronicles the achievements of Eastern medicine, from Byzantium to Central Asia, India and China. Tribute must be paid to the great Samanid library where the young Avicenna discovered the works of Celsius, the great Byzantine surgeon, and the experiences of Al-Kharis, the great Arabic doctor who healed the Prophet Muhammad. While writing his *Canon,* Ibn Sina summarized and analyzed this ocean of knowledge by freeing it from mysticism, and testing and enriching it with his own years of experience.

The *Canon* is the most famous textbook in the history of the teaching of medicine, and it has been the most popular book for five centuries, after the Bible and the Koran. Since the 11th century, the *Canon* has been regarded as the ultimate reference for all medical matters. This extraordinary scientific work was translated into Latin in the 12th century, one hundred years after the death of Ibn Sina. Medieval Europe was experiencing a decline in the field of medicine, but through the *Canon* it was able to access a precious knowledge from the achievements of oriental medicine, and the heritage of the ancient healers. The *Canon* was among the first books to be printed in Venice in the 15th century, soon after the first printing machine was invented. By the 17th century, the *Canon* was printed 40 times, coming second only to the Bible in the number of prints.

For the doctors of Western Europe, this work remained the ultimate reference for medical information untill the beginning of the 18th century when new discoveries challenged the 700 year-old book! The Constitution of Krakow University states that any student studying medicine must know the *Canon*, especially its first part, which contains information on the human organism, methods for diagnosis, and choice of medicine. In Leipzig too, the *Canon* was the foundation of a medical education. Leonardo da Vinci, Michelangelo, and Dante, learned their medicine from the *Canon*.

Avicenna's name was also known in Russia. Russian medieval manuscripts of medicine often quote the "Wisdom of Ovsien" - which was the name given to Ibn Sina by the doctors of Moscow, Kiev, and Novgorod.

In the East, Avicenna is still considered the ultimate reference for medical matters, and healers still use his techniques to cure.

Besides the *Canon*, Avicenna left a series of other works on medicine. These include works written in verses. In his versed works, the scientist created a popular form of sayings, covering various fields of medicine including anatomy, diagnosis, rules for a good diet and a healthy life-style, and rules for good hygiene. Ibn Sina studied the life of centenarians carefully. He was interested in their eating habits and their physical activity. By analyzing his notes he launched a new science called gerontology.

"One who neglects physical exercise is often sick, as the strength in his organs diminishes with inaction."

The discoveries made by Ibn Sina a thousand years ago are still striking. Ibn Sina was the first in the history of medicine to note the affect of the myocardial infarction on other organs of the body. Modern medicine didn't discover this until the 20th century. He was also the first in the history of medicine to predict that the plague was a transmissible disease caused by rats, and the first to describe anthrax, cholera, and leprosy. He made very clear the distinctions between these diseases, and also described their development and cure. According to contemporary neurologists, there isn't much to add to Ibn Sina's description of meningitis. The same goes for his works on diabetes. In addition, Avicenna was the first in the history of medicine to fully describe pleurisy, asthma, and tuberculosis, and establish them separately from lung infections. His description of tuberculosis was so detailed that even with the discovery of x-rays, nothing could be added.

The oriental doctor was also a gifted surgeon. His unique experience as a surgeon, detailed in the *Canon*, served as an example for generations of doctors. He understood the mechanisms of dislocation, and his methods for the diagnosis and cure of bone fractures are still used today. They are called "Ibn Sina methods". The scientist contributed greatly in the fields of eye diseases and eye surgery, and he also made the very precious discovery that the general health of a person is connected to his or her sight. This idea was still being developed in the year 1851! It was in this year that Hemholtz was able to establish direct links between the back of the eye and the sicknesses experienced by a person.

Avicenna also unveiled the mystery of the mysterious disease that terrorized Europe for centuries, rabies. He described the causes, the development, and the cure of the disease. Even though he was respected, his recommendation was regarded with great skepticism; it looked too much like a healer's recipe. Think about it. Avicenna, the educated man and the great scientist, wrote that the best cure for rabies was to drink a beverage made from the kidneys of a dog affected by rabies. Only the 20th century researchers who discovered vaccination confirmed the discovery of this incredible mind. The great doctor also recommended that a patient should drink the juice of goat kidneys to cure night-blindness. This was much criticized at the time, but the doctors of the 20th century proved that goat kidneys contain huge quantities of vitamin A, which helps to cure night-blindness.

Avicenna's sense of observation still strikes his colleagues, ten centuries later. Incredibly, he could differentiate 48 forms of pulsation, with ten different parameters each, 26 forms of breathing, 15 forms of pain, and 9 different types of medical drugs. He was familiar with 12,000 different drugs of mineral origin and 1400 of biological origin. In his *Book on Heart Drugs*, the scientist made the first description in the history of medicine of heart disease, and gave a full description of drugs to be taken for it. In his *Treaty Al-Vakhia*, the compilation of Ibn Sina's first recipes, there is the first mention of elements able to improve memory and concentration, which today are called psycho-stimulants.

None of Ibn Sina illustrious predecessors left any work on psychiatry - neither Hippocratus nor Gatenus. Ibn Sina's experience, echoed in his works, laid the foundations of this science, as well as others, such as psychology, neurology and neurosurgery. The scientist researched in detail the influence of psychic activity on health. He didn't limit himself to theorizing, but conducted experiments using animals. In order to prove the direct connection between the psychic state and the physiological processes taking place in an organism, Ibn Sina conducted an experiment on two sheep. They were placed in different locations and fed with the exact same food. One was placed in a very quiet place, and the other one was placed close to a wolf who was constantly trying to break his chain. The first sheep was eating quietly and gaining weight, whereas the other one, placed in permanent stress, was losing his appetite, and getting worse. It finally died of exhaustion. This experiment proved the scientist's theories about the influence of the soul on the body.

Once Ibn Sina was invited to the palace because the emir's nephew was suffering from a mysterious disease. Avicenna sat by the bed of the patient and asked him details about his health. After listening to the pulse of the young man, he requested the presence of a particular man who was an expert on knowledge of their city. Still feeling the pulse of the patient, he asked the expert to name all of the streets of the city. Avicenna felt that when one particular street was named, the young man's pulse accelerated. He then asked the expert to list all of the houses on that particular street, and once again he felt the young man's pulse accelerate, this time when a particular number was mentioned. Ibn Sina then requested that the expert name all of the inhabitants of that particular house. As soon as the name of a woman was mentioned, the patient started shaking, his pulse went crazy, and he turned red. Immediately, Ibn Sina understood the whole situation. He informed the emir that his nephew was in love, and the only cure was a marriage with his beloved. The boy's parents were relieved to learn that the life of the young man was no longer in danger, and they couldn't hide their admiration for the talented doctor and his refined diagnosis.

This story is true, but their are many false legends and untrue stories attributed to Ibn Sina, an incredibly talented man!

LEONARDO DA VINCI
(1452 - 1519)

History knows no other person so generously endowed with talents by nature. Some writers seriously propose that he was a traveler in time who appeared by accident, and was not able to return back to the future.

The Child of the Renaissance

His personality always captivates me; I never pass up any reading on him that I find. I'm overjoyed that I was lucky enough to have the chance to see his fascinating paintings.

Leonardo da Vinci seems to have been the chosen one. It was as if nature wanted to combine all human talents and abilities in him, to see what the "perfect creation" would be like. All of his talents could have been distributed among dozens of people, and all of these people would have entered history as great musicians, artists, sculptors, mathematicians, astronomers, mechanists, military engineers, opticians, anatomists, physiologists, geologists, and botanists. However, all of these talents belonged to Leonardo da Vinci alone.

Leonardo came into the world during history's greatest period in human creative energy - the Renaissance. On April 15, 1452, a lovely peasant woman named Catherine gave birth to Leonardo in Vinci, a small town near Florence. The boy was as beautiful as Cupid! The father of the boy, the young and successful notary Pietro da Vinci, took his illegitimate child to his home, where Leonardo grew up cherished by the notary's numerous householders. Even Leonardo's stepmothers babied and pampered him. The child learned everything easily, and enjoyed studying very much.

"You are studying as if you were playing," said Leonardo's stepmother Albiera, with delight. Unfortunately, Albiera's was the first death in Leonardo's life. When she caught fever and died, he was left with a feeling of sadness and loss that brought tears to his eyes.

Leonardo's second stepmother's name was Francesca. She had hardly turned 15 when she put on her wedding dress and shared a bed with Pietro da Vinci. When Francesca first met Leonardo, she offered to play hide-and-seek with him. She was so overtaken by the game that she did not notice how much it bored the boy. "When you grow up, dear mother, I will teach you some very interesting things, like geometry," said Leonardo sarcastically to his stepmother, who was a head shorter than him.

With great enthusiasm, Leonardo studied mathematics, Latin, music, and signing, but he was particularly fond of drawing. Leonardo's talent in drawing lead his father to show his work to the Florence painter Andrea del Verrochio. The latter was so astonished by Leonardo's first drawings that he offered to teach Leonardo painting.

Nurturing Talent

In Florence, under the guidance of his teacher, Leonardo studied the whole course of arts for 10 years. The education he obtained at the art workshop played an important role in the development of the young man. He studied along with Petrugino, Boticcelli, and Lorenzo di Crudi, who later became prominent Italian painters.

At the age of twenty Leonardo was proclaimed master. The versatility of his interests, and his inquisitive mind, made him among the most prominent scientists at that time. He frequently met with the teacher of Christopher Columbus, the astronomer, physicist, and natural scientist Count Paolo Toscanelli, and with the mathematician Paolo del Abaco. Leonardo greatly benefited from his acquaintance with Joann Argiropulo, an expert in antiquity, and a professor of the Greek language. Already at that time the young man was trying to closely link arts with science in order to learn the rules of perspective, light, and shadow, and the combination of colors.

At the same time, Leonardo was not a hermit. His passion for arts and science did not overshadow his interest in the other pleasures of life. He was an enthusiastic participant of all celebrations and tournaments. A winning horse racer, he could tame the wildest horse. He could also play the lute remarkably, and he was a matchless dancer, and a gallant cavalier. His elegant hands easily bent a horseshoe, and his timeless beauty and well-proportioned body attracted the admiring glances of women.

I can make light, easily movable bridges, and absolutely indestructible iron carts

By the age of thirty, Leonardo da Vinci became an encyclopedically educated man. His life meant studying and obtaining knowledge of the universe. He devoted himself to creative work, and realized that in order to be able to dedicate himself to science, the arts, and engineering, he needed the patronage of a powerful person. Therefore, all his life Leonardo felt a humiliating dependence on the rich and famous.

In his letter to the Milan duke Ludovico Sforzo, called Moro, Leonardo recommended himself as an engineer who could make "light, easily movable bridges" and who knew various ways to destroy any fort with weapons such as catapults, arrow shooters, bombs and "closed, absolutely indestructible iron carts." At the end of his letter he wrote, "in a time of peace I hope to be able to sustain competition with anyone in the field of architecture, using marvel, bronze or clay, as well as in the fine arts. I will do nothing inferior to anybody who wishes to compete with me."

On order from Ludovico Moro, Leonardo da Vinci created a grandiose project for the reconstruction of the city fort and the famous Milano Cathedral. There he also created his painting masterpieces "Madonna in Grotto" and the "Secret Evening". In Milan, Leonardo da Vinci worked for 16 years on the horse mounted statue of duke Francesco Sforzo. The statue was admired by his contemporaries, but did not survive. Leonardo did not have time to make it in bronze, and the clay model was destroyed at the French siege of Milan in 1500. In the same way, dozens of Leonardo da Vinci's paintings and drawings have been irrevocably lost. This is an irreplaceable loss for humankind.

The shift from light to shadow is similar to smoke

Leonardo valued fine arts higher that any other occupation, and by the end of his life he was most famous as a great painter. He considered fine arts to be a science, since "its final result is a subject of visual ability." He created the concept of "aerial perspective," and as no one before, he was able to express how depth envelops objects with the shifting "smoke" of light and shadow. Leonardo's soft manner of painting distinguished him from his contemporaries, with their strict approach to form and color.

To develop his knowledge of the proportions of the human body, Leonardo seriously studied anatomy. He believed that without an excellent knowledge of anatomy and physiology, one couldn't realistically depict a human being. He needed to capture accurate anatomy and physiology in his paintings in order to work for an expressiveness of images, and a "uniformity with nature."

Leonardo's works brought him world fame. They are exhibited in various museums today. The *Madonna Litta* and the *Madonna Benoit,* exhibited in the graceful Italian Halls of the Hermitage Museum, always attract admirers. Visitors inevitably move in to ponder up close the masterpieces created by the great Leonardo.

Madonna Litta moved to the Hermitage from the Milan collection of Marchioness Litta, in 1885. It belongs to Leonardo da Vinci's Milan period, a period of blossoming in his talent. *Madonna Benoit (Madonna with Flower)* is a small painting that was obtained by the Hermitage in 1914 from the collection of Benoit, the family who gave Russia many prominent artists, architects, and musicians. Until the 19th century this remarkable work was attributed to the great Verrochio. Leonardo had a great respect for his teacher, and appreciated him very much, but he liked to say, "If a student does not outperform his teacher, he must not be a very good student at all." After a thorough analysis conducted in 1990, the *Madonna with Flower* was recognized as belonging to Leonardo da Vinci.

The secret of the *Madonna Benoit* has finally been solved, but for five centuries researchers have been trying to resolve another enigma: the mysterious smile of Leonardo's *Mona Lisa.* There are many propositions as to who is depicted in the portrait. Some art historians believe that it was the portrait of a Florence lady made on order from Juliano Medici, the son of the late Lorenzo the Magnificent. The majority of experts share this opinion, but it has not been confirmed by historical documents.

Why name the painting *Mona Lisa*? The rich moneylender Francesco Gioconda had a beautiful wife named Mona Lisa. When Francesco brought his wife before the painter, Leonardo requested that he provide singers, musicians, and comedians, to support the mood of the lady. Francesco did not know that

Leonardo had courted and fallen in love with her. There are many propositions about Leonardo's relationship with Mona Lisa. Undoubtedly, she played a great role in his life, and inspired him to great creative endeavors.

The portrait of *Mona Lisa* continues to enchant new generations of admirers. None of the portraitists of the 15th century managed to express as exquisitely the internal life of a model. The young woman in the *Mona Lisa* is looking out at us with the wonderful calm of a person who understands the beauty of the world around her. This is an understanding that Leonardo most likely shared.

The internal world of a person is the most elevated and engaging enigma. To understand it and express it to people - to show people how inimitably beautiful they are inside - was the main goal of Leonardo da Vinci as a painter. He was a person passionately in love with life, in all of its expressions.

Finding something divine in being human was also one of Leonardo's incredible goals. Look at his *Secret Evening*. Is it not a depiction of our life? A person who has just taken a drink from a cup is putting it on the table and turning his head towards someone who is speaking. Another person, with his fingers interlaced and eyebrows fixed, is turning to his companion, while his companion is lifting open palms with his shoulders shrugged, and his mouth opened in amazement. Another person has a knife in one hand, and a half-cut loaf of bread in another, and is speaking in the ear of someone who is turning to him. The person turning to him has just overturned a cup on the table.

Today Leonardo's *Secret Evening* is considered a masterpiece of the world. It has a rich and inimitable combination of light, shadow, colors, and expression of air, and an exquisiteness of perspective. The result is an intimate and inspired work. A witness said that while Leonardo was working on this Biblical canvas, he "did not let the brush out of his hand from sunrise to sunset, and stood by the picture forgetting about food and drink."

Talent plus work is what it takes to make a masterpiece. No other recipe has been discovered yet.

Judgement from an enemy is more useful than admiring praise from friends.

This bitter axiom came to be understood by Leonardo da Vinci through personal experience. At the courts of Italian and French rulers, Leonardo was greatly esteemed as a prominent mechanic, architect, military engineer, sculptor, artist, and musician. However, the fulfillment of small caprices - like the organization of ceremonies, or fireworks - burdened the master and distracted him from his serious work. Leonardo's life consisted of endless moving in search of minimum distraction.

When Leonardo served Pope Leo X in the Vatican, he became keen in anatomy. He tried to link the physiological structures of various organs with their functions, and frequently dissected and analyzed human corpses at St. Peter's hospital. For that, even the Papal guardsmen were afraid of him. At nights, while standing on watch, they often saw Leonardo going to the local morgue, lighting his way with a flashlight. As the guardsman drank wine, their imaginations filled with the possibilities of deviltry in Leonardo's trips to the morgue. Somebody started a rumor that the scientist was cutting out dead children's hearts and making a wonderful drug for witchcraft. Others said that Leonardo da Vinci was eating human meat! (In fact, during the last thirty years of his life, the scientist was a vegetarian. "It is a great atrocity to eat animals that we are not able to create ourselves," said Leonardo.)

The wild rumors, added with other nonsense, reached the Pope. Leo X did not believe the absurdities, but he noted that if Leonardo was provoking stupid rumors in the capital of the Christian world, then he deserved reprimand. The superintendent of the hospital was forced to prohibit Leonardo from any further experiments. Thus, some of Leonardo's great initiatives were broken because of human pettiness.

Fortunately, Leonardo had a diverse spectrum of interests! The tireless scientist studied parallel acoustics, the laws of the proliferation of sound in a liquid environment, and conducted experiments on the study of a bird's flight. The sketches made by Leonardo depict the wing of a planer, a parachute, and a helicopter. In one of his notebooks, the scientist wrote under a small sketch of a flying mechanism, "Man, like a great bird, will take his first flight on the back of an admirable swan. He will amaze the world and fill books with his great experiences - bringing an eternal glory to his motherland!"

Leonardo da Vinci was convinced that one day man would discover the secret of flight. He thought that this moment of discovery "was not centuries away, but very close, somewhere nearby." He probably assumed that the next generation would have the same resourcefulness as he. Alas, humankind is not so spoiled with geniuses.

Sometimes people do not appreciate geniuses. Extraordinary thinking frightens dilettantes. Leonardo was blamed for witchcraft, sorcery, blasphemy, heresy, and insult to religion. The accusations were encouraged by the sarcastic remarks of his jealous competitor, Michelangelo. The latter was announcing everywhere that a kitchen cook was a better expert in the arts than that "lousy violin player from Milan." At first Leonardo took offense, but such unfair slander developed another talent in him, and he became a fable writer.

With his characteristic brilliance, Leonardo staged a few dozen satirical shows. They are all very sardonic, with philosophic connotations. "The stream brought so many stones and earth into its waterbed, that it was forced to leave," was the brief theme of one of the fables. Another theme was, "A piece of paper saddened when it saw that it was covered with ink, until the ink told the paper that exactly because of the letters written on its surface, the paper would be preserved for many years." Such fables, called fazzetias, remind one of Bocaccio's novellas.

Leonardo depicted overzealous clergman with the same sarcastic wit. The following is an example of this:

"On Good Friday, a churchman was walking around his parish, and he dropped by a painter's shop (meant to be Leonardo's shop, of course). The churchman sprinkled holy water onto the artist's fresh paintings, and the artist was outraged. 'Why spoil a work of art?' he asked.

The Churchman responded, 'It was a blessing, and one who gives a blessing will be blessed a hundred fold.'

What could the poor artist do? When the churchman stepped out of the shop, the painter came to the window, splashed a bucket of water on the churchman, and said, 'Here is your hundred fold for your blessing that spoiled my paintings!'"

After such fables, the "enlightened patron of arts," Pope Leo X , rushed to get rid of Leonardo. Leonardo was forced to leave Italy, and although the royalty of France respectfully welcomed him, they very soon became suspicious of his scientific explorations. Kings, after all, are not geniuses.

Soon a real misfortune befell Leonardo: his right hand

was paralyzed. Because he could no longer paint as he used to, Leonardo da Vinci started a new life in which he became completely overtaken with science and engineering experiments. He finished his discourses on anatomy and wrote his topical works *On the Nature of Water*, and *On Various Mechanisms*. He developed a project for connecting the Sona and Luarrea rivers with a canal, in order to irrigate a large agricultural area. One hundred years after Leonardo's death, the canal was built by French engineers, according to Leonardo's sketches.

Shortly before his death Leonardo da Vinci wrote, "I know very well that some arrogant men think they can criticize me. They say I am not well read, but I can answer them, 'You have the right to learn other people's works, so shouldn't I have the right to do things my own way?' They do not understand that my writings are not taken from other people's work, but from my own practical experiments. An experiment is a teacher that I can refer to at any time. Science is the captain, and practice is the soldier."

When composing his will, the great old Leonardo tried to oversee everything . He insisted on paying for 500 candles to be at his funeral. King Francesco himself would probably wish to see him off on his last journey, and it would not be appropriate to make the king pay for candles, flowers, and other funeral miscellany.

Before his death Leonardo came up with many maxims, including, "Necessity is the instructor of nature, and its bridle," and, "The one who argues using his experience, is using his memory more than his mind." The 67 year-old master uttered his genius expressions with ease and, as usual, inspiration, to his disciple, Francesco Melci.

Leonardo da Vinci died on May 2, 1519 in France. His last phrase was: "Please forgive me for what I did not do..."

Shortly before his death, Leonardo asked that his writings be sent to Italy. Clearly he had missed his home country very much.

Life is Motion

Leonardo's versatile talent enriched almost all of the sciences of his time. Unfortunately, the scientist did not have time to accomplish all of his plans. The scientist's intellectual treasures were recorded in his numerous notebooks. In these notebooks Leonardo put his thoughts, technical ideas, drawings, sketches, extracts, and mathematical calculations.

Leonardo considered science to be a powerful tool of cognition, especially mathematics. "No human research," he wrote, " can claim to be an authentic science if it is not backed by mathematical proof." The consistent application of a mathematical method enabled Leonardo to make a number of important discoveries in anatomy, geology, botany, and, most of all, physics. It was because he knew modern mathematics so completely that he was able to solve the problems of perspective and composition. "The whole philosophy," wrote Leonardo, in objection to various idealists, "is written in one grandiose book that is always before us; I am talking about the universe."

All his life Leonardo persistently studied this universal book. Hundreds of discoveries have been catalogued by his extraordinary mind. For example, he identified fluctuation as the universal movement of nature. At a time of church obscurantism, this great man loudly stated that light, sound, smell, heat, and magnetism, all moved only in waves. It wasn't until the 19th century that others seriously researched this phenomenon, the way Leonardo did in the 15th century! Leonardo may not have proved this phenomenon, but he knew it for sure. "Movement is the cause of any expression of life," he wrote when he was young.

Mathematics and engineering helped Leonardo to develop his talents as a military engineer. He constructed defense facilities, and designed siege machines and weapons. Having thoroughly studied the art of making cannons, he designed many automatic weapons, such as arrow shooters, bombs, and explosives.

According to Vasari, Leonardo's biographer, the scientist was very interested in hydro-engineering. Leonardo was the first in history to ask himself "how to use the Arno river to link Pisa and Florence with a canal," in order to improve the freight turnover and supply raw materials to mills. "He made sketches of yard machines and other equipment that could be started by the force of water," created designs of water and wind mills to generate energy, and dreamed about the use of solar energy. He conducted endless experiments with various plants, studying the influence of the sun, water, and soil on them.

Leonardo's contemporaries considered his interests to be mere fantasies, but we know that he was peeking into our century. The sketches of helicopters, planers, automatic looms, first step mechanisms, submarines, and various optical instruments, made by Leonardo da Vinci in the 15th century, are his gifts to the 20th century. By predicting and anticipating many of the greatest discoveries of later centuries, he astonished scientists, far into the future, and still amazes scientists today. Leonardo da Vinci was the first in history to formulate the law of hydrostatics and friction. He came up with the concept of a center of gravity in objects, and came very close to explaining the static moment. He wrote about capillarity and the diffraction of light, and anticipated the discovery of the law of preservation of energy, by ruling out the possibility of a "perpetuum mobile." Leonardo created a great number of new mechanical, physical, and chemical instruments and test tools, including proportional compasses and anemometers. In astronomy, Leonardo theorized a heliocentric structure of the universe 50 years before Copernicus wrote his discourse on the spinning of the Earth. Leonardo also announced that the universe and space were endless.

Having studied the composition of the human eye, Leonardo made correct guesses about the nature of binocular vision. He came up with a theory based on "vital air" (oxygen), anticipating the discoveries of Louvazirre by three centuries. Leonardo was also a century ahead of Cardon, the designer of the obscure chamber, which is used in photography. Three centuries before Sussore, Leonardo invented the hygrometer, an instrument for measuring air humidity. He also introduced the concepts of plus and minus to mathematics, and created the map of the New World from descriptions made by Amerigo Vespucci.

Leonardo created everywhere, and at any time. Many of his scientific solutions were not understood, and therefore remained unimplemented. For almost 500 years researchers have been trying to understand his scientific work, original engineering, technical conclusions, and mathematical truths.

Leonardo's intellectual power, his outstanding discoveries, and his great artistic talents, amaze the human imagination. The people of the Renaissance perceived him as the personification of ideal human qualities. He remains an ideal for us, now standing on the threshold of the XXI century.

"The artist who never doubts in anything, does not achieve much," Leonardo used to say. These are great words. No matter how clever we may think we are, and no matter how strongly we believe in our exquisite taste and perfect intuition, it does no harm to step aside, look around, and think again.

We can learn this by studying the life of the great Leonardo da Vinci.

JOHANNES KEPLER
(1571- 1630)

This scientist exemplifies an unbending determination and an unwavering devotion. Despite all of the misfortunes of his life, Johannes Kepler managed to prove the theory of Copernicus, which places the sun rather than the earth, at the center of our universe.

Not strong enough to be a Landskhniecht!

Fate was not merciful to the German scientist Kepler. The whole of his life was filled with poverty, misfortune, and religious persecution.

Johannes Kepler was born on December 27, 1571 in Wuertemberg, Germany. Johannes' father, Henrich Kepler, who considered himself to be a nobleman, was the owner of a small village tavern. He was also a troublemaker and a rascal. Johannes' mother, Catherine, was an uneducated, scandalous, ill-mannered, and drinking woman. For that, and the fact that as a child she had stayed with an aunt who was later burned at the stake for witchcraft, fellow villagers called her "witch". They seriously believed that she practiced sorcery.

Johannes nearly died at birth, and his health remained bad throughout his life. When he was four, Catherine left him at home and went to the Netherlands in search of her husband. Johannes' father was serving there as a landskniecht - a mercenary soldier. He was fighting in wars and enjoying himself, of course, without dropping a line to his wife. The brave soldier never even remembered his son. In the meantime, Johannes caught smallpox. He barely survived the illness. That was not the last time. Once again, when Johannes was thirteen, it seemed like only a miracle could save him from death. However, his weak body would not give up. Johannes struggled to survive as if he did not want to leave the world without fulfilling his glorious mission.

When Johannes was six, he attended a primary school. He had great success in reading, writing and arithmetic. His glorious father by that time was back from the war with more money wasted on drink than brought home. His heroic deeds did not promote the family from semi-beggarly living. In the evenings everyone was busy with backbreaking work, including the future academician, who waited on tables in the village tavern until his legs ached. A moment of relief and enjoyment would come only at night, when he returned to his books.

The family had a joyless life. Ever drunk, his parents often quarreled. The family was in need of the most essential things. The unhealthy boy did not live up to his parent's expectations because he was not strong enough to be a landskniecht. As a result, he felt unneeded.

Because of his weak health, Johannes could not learn a handicraft or do agricultural work, so he was given to the theological school under the Maulbourn monastery. The boy visibly cheered up at this move. It was there that Kepler exhibited his extraordinary capabilities. He was noticed, distinguished, and treated kindly - for the first time in life. Soon, for his diligence, he was sent to Teubengen theological college, and within two years, in the year 1591, he acquired the qualification of a teacher and entered the Teubengen Academy - the highest theological school of Wuertemberg.

Kepler's luck seemed to be turning.

Astrology is an Illegitimate Daughter of Astronomy

Wicked fate took pity, and helped Johannes meet Michael Meustlin, the professor of astronomy at the academy.

An excellent lecturer, an outstanding instructor, and the author of many research works, M. Menstlin seemed to know everything about the celestial sky. It was at this time that Kepler developed a special interest in astronomy. The young man's zeal was noticed by his teacher. Soon Mestlin started teaching the talented young man at his own house. Many years later, Johannes remembered the dusky quietness of Mestlin's office with a special sympathy. He never forgot what he owed his teacher. From M. Mestlin, Kepler learned about the theory of Nicolas Copernicus. After he thoroughly studied the theory, he became a hot-blooded supporter of the heliocentric idea of the universe, in which the sun is the center of the universe around which all of the planets spin.

Oh, youth! Your beliefs are naive, but pure and innocent. Your noble conscience passionately clings to new ideas, and your mind absorbs them like a sponge. How important it is not to spill this juvenile passion, but to carry its romance all through life. Only one out of a hundred-thousand manages to do so. Kepler was one of these such people.

When he graduated from the Academy, Johannes' diploma read, "No doubt must be cast on his outstanding abilities in various sciences, and his eloquence in public speaking." This diploma was not at all good for a theological career. To prepare for a career, Johannes should have admired Copernicus less. It was then that Johannes' reputed teacher came to his aide. Thanks to Mestlin's petitioning, Kepler was given a position as a teacher of mathematics and morals at the grammar school of the ever green town of Gratz. Later, he taught his favorite discipline, astronomy, there.

Unfortunately, the salary of a teacher existed only on paper. The payroll was irregular, and the delays were often long. To make a living, the young astronomer composed horoscopes. To his friends he wrote, "It is better to chart almanacs with fortune telling, than to ask for alms. Astrology is astronomy's daughter, although an illegitimate one. Is it not a natural thing when the daughter feeds her mother, who otherwise would starve to death?"

In 1594 in Gratz, Kepler charted a new Gregorian calendar. Its chronology was organized in accordance with a schedule introduced by Pope Gregory XIII in 1582. In other words, Johannes was responsible for calendar reform. Such things are not welcomed by everyone. For example, the Protestants, Kepler's co-religionists, were outraged.

"We consider the Roman Pope to be a roaring lion. If we accept his calendar, then soon we will have to go to church by his directions," they said.

It is hard to tell today what the Protestants did not like about the new calendar. Kepler worked it out very diligently. He did not forget to mention the weather forecast, so important for farmers. Most importantly, he mentioned various folk predictions, without which some impressionable people couldn't fall asleep. He also could not resist the temptation of sharing his astrological forecast for the nearest future, which although it did not promise anything good, also predicted no end to the world. It seemed to say to people that they should live, and try to be happy!

At that time, astrology was considered a serious science. The French astrologer L. Arago wrote, "They say Kepler believes in horoscopes himself." Indeed, if Kepler composed them, then he probably believed them, but this was not his main occupation. Once, he gave the following explanation for his astrology: "The person who is searching for truth needs at least two things to be able to freely devote himself to his occupation; he needs food and a dwelling. The one who has nothing is a slave of everything. If I compose calendars and almanacs, this is of course, forgive me God, a slavery. Should I rid myself of this at least for some time, I will have to go into a slavery much more humiliating."

Soon Kepler married a young widow, Barbara Muller. In

all respects she was an educated and attractive woman, but their happiness did not last for a long time. The Austrian archduke came of age, and started trying to exterminate the "Lutheran heresy." All Protestants were ordered to leave the town immediately, on penalty of death. Kepler was a Lutheran.

Proposals from local officials for Kepler to enter into an arrangement with government circles, were dismissed. Kepler belonged to the Lutheran church, and he could not feign. The Jesuits, who valued Kepler as a competent astrologer, petitioned for him, but this did not help. Kepler had to flee to one of the Protestant states of Germany, where he received an invitation to go to Prague from the famous astronomer, Tycho Brahe. This invitation marked the beginning of their uneasy collaboration.

"Tycho is a person with whom one cannot live, without accepting insult," wrote Kepler. He knew that he had to put up with Tycho. At that time Brahe was considered the most prominent astronomer. He was patronized by the King of Denmark, Frederick II, who never refused him in financial subsidies. Thanks to that support, Tycho had built the most prestigious astronomic observatory in the world, on the island of Khvene at Uranibohrg, near Copenhagen. During 21 years of continual observations, Tycho collected unique material on the celestial position of stars and planets, and shared his knowledge with the young Kepler. Johannes was promised an excellent salary, but the treasury there was also empty, and he was not paid for months.

Tycho Brahe promised Kepler the title of "Imperial Mathematician" under the condition that he work along with Brahe on the new tables of planet movements. However, the views of the two scientists did not coincide. Kepler believed that the basis of all calculations should be the system of Copernicus, the heliocentric model, while Tycho Brahe believed that the earth was the center of the universe, around which the sun, the moon, and all the other planets spun. Tycho demanded that Kepler use the earth-centered model of the universe as the basis for the new tables, but the two scientists continued to have conflicting views, so the work did not progress.

The New Astronomy, Free of Charge

When Tycho died, Kepler was appointed "Imperial Mathematician," and the composition of the tables of planet movement were charged to him. Nine long years of his observations of Mars, and also the data collected before him, enabled him to verify that Mars' real orbit was an ellipse. According to Kepler, he contemplated this subject so much that he nearly went mad.

In 1609 Kepler published his book, *The New Astronomy*, in Prague. Since then the heliocentric model of the universe has been firmly grounded.

Johannes Kepler came up with the following two laws of planetary motion for the heliocentric universe:

1. All planets move along ellipses, and the sun is located in one of the focuses of these ellipses.

2. The radius vector from the Sun to a planet covers equal areas at equal periods of time.

The first copy of the book, with Kepler's dedication, was sent to the Emperor, but Kepler still was not paid his due salary for several years. His family lived in hunger and poverty, and Kepler had to take occasional paid work.

Soon the war broke out, bringing epidemics. Kepler's wife and three children died. The new emperor approved him as the "Imperial Mathematician" but still did not pay him. There was only one thing Kepler could do. He had to accept any job that would pay him. The prominent scientist, and the father of international discoveries, had to move to Austria where he was promised a teaching job at the grammar school in the town of Linz.

The Witch's Son

At first Kepler's life in Linz was better than in Prague. Johannes got married again and had children, but he was still a Protestant, and the Catholics of Linz were not friendly to him. Soon they started a rumor that Kepler was a "witch's son". In 1615 Kepler's mother had been accused of witchcraft and imprisoned. She was sentenced to be burned at the stake. Kepler petitioned, and wrote letters for several years to save his mother from this terrible execution. The trial process lasted for six years. Finally, in 1621, Kepler managed to obtain a permission for the release of his elderly mother, saving her from torture. Although Catherine was not convicted, Kepler was still called the "witch's son".

Persecution made Kepler's life unbearable, but he still found strength for his work. How could one not be amazed by the unbending determination of Kepler? Under such conditions he managed to publish new scientific research works: *The Concise Copernican Astronomy*, and *The Harmony of the World*, in five volumes. In the latter, Kepler formulated the third law of celestial mechanics. According to that law, "The square of turn periods (time) of planets around the Sun are proportional to cubes of large semi axles of their orbits." Kepler rechecked his calculations 70 times "to make sure of their accuracy." There are seven volumes of such calculations. Still, Kepler was not paid. The family led a semi-starved life, and had no means to leave the hostile town.

In 1627 Kepler's house was besieged by a street crowd. There were threats addressed to the witch's son, and calls to execute the heretics. It seemed that the crowd was going to break the doors down. Kepler's wife and children were terrified by the shouts, so they began praying to God. They could not believe it when suddenly the street noise disappeared. Kepler's title, "Imperial Mathematician," saved them. The authorities calmed the fanatics down, but for how long? The Kepler family did not feel safe until they had escaped to the emperor's residence.

The Legacy of 22 Florins in Cash

Soon Kepler finished his fundamental work, *The Rudolfian Tables,* based on calculations of planet movements made by Tycho, which Kepler had continued and developed. The tables explained the theory of eclipses, and provided a very simple method of identifying the point on the earth from which one could observe certain phases of eclipses. The calculations made by Kepler, on the basis of the *Rudolfian Tables,* indicated that Venus was to go along the Solar disk in 1631. Kepler wrote about this in his brochure, *On rare and phenomenal events of 1631.* The scientist himself did not live to see his prediction come true, but after it happened, the scientific world called the brochure a benchmark of scientific calculation.

At that time Kepler was also working in optics. He introduced the concept of the light ray, studied light refraction, and designed the telescope in the form in which it is still used today in many places. Kepler's ideas significantly influenced crystallography.

Kepler's contemporaries underestimated him as a mathematician. He was an expert in methods of approximated calculations, which he created himself. Kepler made great contributions to the theory of conical links, and the theory of logarithms. In connection with the calculation of the volumes of some objects, he envisioned integral calculations. He also contributed to the design of the first calculation machine.

Kepler's last years were spent in poverty. To be fair it should be mentioned that various rulers of different countries offered him their patronage many times. In 1621, the government of the Venice Republic offered the famous astronomer and mathematician an attractive and lucrative position at the head of the astronomy department in Padua University. Galileo himself worked in that department until 1610, but Kepler refused. He acknowledged the benefits of the offer but said, "I am used to speaking the truth, and therefore I do not want to step on fire like Jordano Bruno."

Was he frightened? Maybe. The fires of the Inquisition were burning at that time across the whole of Italy. Rome had just condemned Copernicus's theory. It was better to be hungry than to be burned. At approximately the same time, Johannes refused the invitation to go to England. What was it that kept him in his ungrateful country that time? I have no answer to that question. After all, he was in need of the most essential things, such as food, clothes, ink, feathers for writing, and paper. Once he interrupted his research and wrote a fantastic novel called *The Dream*. It was about the dwellers of the Moon, who lived in cold and dark caves without envy of, or hope to see life on the earth. Kepler hoped to get a good royalty for the book, but he did not live to see his novel released. Kepler's son published it only four years after his father's death, under the title, *The Dream (a posthumous novel on moon astronomy)*.

The scientist traveled from Linz to Regensburg many

times with the hope that he would receive at least part of the salary that he had earned in many years. To save money, he traveled on a horseback. He made his last 400 kilometer trip in the late autumn of 1630. He caught a cold on the way, and when he arrived in Regensburg he had to take a bed.

The great astronomer died in a bad fever at the age of 59. One of his biographers wrote that his numerous children received a legacy of 22 florins, 2 shirts, 57 copies of *Ethemerids*, and 16 copies of the *Rudolfian Tables*. They also received 30 huge research works composed in many volumes, and an unpaid salary of 29 thousand florins, which they never received.

This was Kepler's earthly gratitude. One has only to believe in heavenly gratitude and blessing. Is there no justice in the universe?

Johannes Kepler had an incredibly difficult life - a half-starved existence, religious persecutions, absurd accusations, horrors of war, and the untimely and unjustified death of family. Still, he managed to leave human kind a generous legacy of enlightenment!

Johannes was an inexhaustible worker that, in spite of hard blows of fate, devoted himself to science. The formulation of the three famous laws of planetary motion in the solar system could be written in just three lines, but it took Johannes Kepler eighteen years of hard work, filled with observations and research, to formulate them. His works laid the foundation for theoretical astronomy, and cleared a path for the study of the gravitation between celestial bodies. Without this, our entry into space would have been impossible.

MIKHAILO LOMONOSOV
(1711 - 1765)

This Primosk self-made man became a prominent Russian scientist and encyclopedist. Mikhailo Lomonosov is also known throughout the world as a physicist, astronomer, geologist, technologist, geographer, poet, painter, philologist, historian, and astronomer. In all of these fields, this great scientist depicted his versatile talent in bright colors.

What do I admire the most about this remarkable person? Of course, the versatility of his talents. The diversity of his gifts could be compared to that of Leonardo da Vinci, but what is more noble about Lomonosov is his persistence in gaining the education needed to indulge these gifts. What talent and will it must have taken for the son of an illiterate fisherman from a remote northern village, to accomplish his dream of a career in science.

The Gates of Learning

Mikhailo Lomonosov was born on November 8, 1711 in the village of Denisovka. He was born to a wealthy family that lived on one of the islands of northern Dvina, near the town of Kholmogory of Arkhangelsk gubernia. The family owned a large land plot, but the main source of their income was fishing.

The Russian north nurtures strong characters, as the severe climate prevents a comfortable life. Perpetual difficulties and dangers encourage only people who do not fear hardships, and will tenaciously fight for what they want. Children in Pomor (northern seafaring) families were brought up in a strict, but dignified manner. Raised with hard work, they grew up strong and healthy.

Since Mikhailo turned ten he was taken fishing in the White and Barents seas with his father, Vasiliy Dorofeyich Lomonosov. On their frail ship the fishermen often went as far as the eternal ice, at 70 degrees of northern latitude. The Lomonosov's had a camp there where they fished and hunted walrus. The journey was long - one thousand kilometers - and it took more than a month. While fishing, the Pomors formed teams in which the teens worked side by side with the adults, on the ships as well as on the seashore.

Sailing on the severe northern seas was a permanent risk. Fishing, sea hunting, and the northern climate, strengthened the young Lomonosov, and enhanced his self-confidence, while developing his intellectual skills. During the long sea journeys he saw icebergs, ebbs and flows, and fantastic northern lights. These majestic natural scenes greatly impressed Mikhailo, and boosted his urge to understand the causes of such phenomenon. At the Vavchug docks, the boy heard stories about how the Czar Peter built a ship with his hands and nearly died during a terrible storm. The image of the Czar as a great patriot and workman stayed in his mind forever. Mikhailo also visited the Solovetskyie islands, where he and his father delivered bread and food. The Antonievo-Syiskyi Monastery was famous for its library and works of art. In Arkhangelsk Mikhailo saw foreign ships at the Gostinyi dvor, a hotel where foreign sailors lived, and also saw the neat houses of the German Town, populated by Germans, Danes, Dutch, and Swedes. Such experiences expanded Lomonosov's horizons, and boosted his curiosity. Lomonosov later recalled that fishing trips with his father were the best part of his childhood.

The Lomonosov's fished from early spring until early polar autumn, and spent long winters at home. Their neighbors were the Shubin family. They were literate people who had books, and were fond of reading. Mikhailo would run to their house at every chance he could. He very quickly learned how to read and write, and when he was 11 he learned grammar and arithmetic. However, after he had read all of his neighbor's books and counted all of the fish in the freezer, what was there to do?

The largest library in Kholmogory belonged to the Dudin family. There, Lomonosov saw his first secular books. These were, *Grammar* by Meletyi Smotritskyi, *Psaltyr Rifmotvornoya* by Semyon Polotskyi, and *Arithmetic* by Leontyi Magnitskyi. When he opened these books for the first time, he was completely overwhelmed by how much he could learn.

Arithmetic taught him how to calculate with both whole and fractional numbers, and offered the fundamentals of algebra, geometry, trigonometry, engineering, astronomy, navigation, and meteorology. Mikhailo persuaded the Dudins to give him the books, and he never went anywhere without them. Soon he learned them by heart. Later he would call them, "The gates of learning."

The books awakened the boy's passion for reading and studying. He was less interested in fiction, and more attracted by the books that fed his intellect. From the local churchman, he learned that the majority of scientific books were written in Latin, and Latin could be learned only in St. Petersburg, Moscow, or Kiev. The young man decided that he had to study in one of these cities.

By then his home life was gradually deteriorating. His mother had died, and his stepmother, a wicked and envious woman, (just like a character from Russian fairy tales) disliked her stubborn stepson. She thought he was just wasting his time studying books. Lomonosov later recalled with bitterness that because of her, he was forced "to read and study in lonely places, and to endure cold and frost." Since Lomonosov could only study in the winter time, and in the beginning of spring before the Lomonosov's went fishing and sea hunting, he could only imagine what it was like to go to school year round. Mikhailo was also the only son in the family. His father hoped to transfer the whole household to Mikhailo. So, when Mikhailo turned 19, his father asked him to get married. He thought that if his son got married, he would forget about books and other "trifles."

The young Lomonosov could not accept such a stay-at-home plan. The doors of knowledge were already opened to him, and he was dreaming of learning the sciences. Therefore, he decided to secretly leave home. With the help of a friend, he managed to obtain his passport from the Kholmogory administrative chancellery. Foma Shubnyi lent him three rubles, a whole fortune at that time. All Mikhailo had to do was to wait for the right moment to come.

One day the village fishermen were going to Moscow with a caravan of fish. In the morning, when the fishermen moved off, Mikhailo impatiently followed the last sledge of the caravan with his eyes. At night, while everyone was sleeping, he took his books, put on two shirts and a coat, put on two huge skies, and set off after the caravan.

He reached the caravan, loaded with mountains of frozen fish, after only three days. He was seventy kilometers away from home. After three weeks, in early January, he arrived in Moscow.

Look at that idiot who came to learn Latin at the age of 20.

The year 1731 marked the beginning of a new age in the life of Mikhailo Lomonosov. His life as a scientific scholar had begun.

There was nobody in Moscow to look out for the young northern fisherman. He could only hope for help from his fellow villagers, who were there to sell fish. They were greatly impressed by the young man's enthusiasm to learn. It was something unusual in their community, but also deserving of respect. They could do nothing but help Mikhailo. The Pomor fishermen decided to find him an appropriate school.

The scientific language at that time was Latin, so Lomonosov applied for admission at the Slavic-Greek-Latin Academy, the only school that taught Latin in Moscow. The Academy produced highly educated clergy. The demand for educated people at that time was so great that the students of the Academy were recruited, even before their graduation, to work for various scientific expeditions. The Academy was closed to the children of peasants, so Mikhailo had to conceal his real lineage. He said that he was the son of an impoverished Kholmogory nobleman.

Although Mikhailo could read and write, and knew the fundamentals of mathematics, he was sent to the first grade. It was at this level that students learned the fundamentals of Latin. Lomonosov was almost twenty, and he was the oldest student in the primary grade. "Look at that idiot who came to learn Latin at 20," he often heard voices saying.

It was hard for a big fellow to live on the small student allowance of 3 kopecks per day. Sometime his fellow villagers would visit him and tell him that his father was looking forward to his return so that he could pass over to him the family property. Despite the fact that Mikhailo often went to classes nearly fainting from starvation, he would not give up. Later Lomonosov recalled, "Having the allowance of only one altyn per day, one could not afford more than some bread and a glass of kvass. The rest was to be spent on paper, footwear, and other needs. I lived this way for five years and did not give up my studies".

Mikhailo's natural intellectual abilities, rare talent, and incredible diligence, enabled him to learn Latin and to complete three grades of the Academy in the first year. After that he learned Greek. The Academy did not allocate much attention to the natural sciences in which Lomonosov was especially interested. Therefore, he had to start studying them independently. The young man spent all of his time in libraries, where he read Latin and Greek writers, and Prussian books that were both printed and hand written. He studied mathematics, geography, and history, and also mastered poetry and oratory techniques. To earn some money, he also served at the Zakonospasskyi Monastery and taught the children of clergymen.

When the expedition to the Trans-Caspian steppes asked for an "educated churchman," the rector of the Academy recommended Mikhailo. Just before graduating, Lomonosov learned that every student's lineage was to be examined by a special state commission. Without waiting for his lie to be discovered, Lomonosov frankly told his professors the story of his entrance into the Academy. The professors were outraged; the son of a peasant was denied access to the holy ordain. However, Mikhailo's frank confession, and his outstanding academic achievement, helped him avoid being expelled from the school. Soon Lomonosov was sent to the Saint Petersburg Academy of Science, where he would become one of their most brilliant students.

The Royal Hussar Spoke In Iambs

In those days, Russian expeditions to Siberia desperately needed chemists, metallurgists, and mining specialists. In less than six months, Lomonosov was sent to Germany, along with the best students of the Saint Petersburg Academy, to study metallurgy and mining. First he would go to Marburg and take courses in mathematics, physics, chemistry, and geography with the famous professor Wolf, and then he would continued his education in Freiburg with the famous Heinkel, professor of metallurgy, chemistry, and mineralogy.

Lomonosov learned much in those years. Professor Christian Wolf represented a scholastic ideal for many students. There were no vacant seats in the auditorium during his classes. He lectured in 16 disciplines: general mathematics, algebra, astronomy, physics, optics, mechanics, military and civil architecture, logic, metaphysics, moral philosophy, politics, natural law, geography, chronology, and literature. The curriculum also included a course of theoretical chemistry taught by professor Duizing.

Lomonosov spent three years in Marburg. There he married Elisabeth-Christian Zilch, the youngest daughter of a respected city council member and beer brewer. She was a modest, delightful, and good-natured woman.

Mikhailo's education in Freiburg with the famous professor Heinkel was very fruitful. He studied mineralogy, mining, engineering, and the structures of various crystals. There he also became strong in chemistry. The young scientist developed his own scientific views, different from traditional views, and those views did always coincide with his professor's.

In May of 1740, Lomonosov left Freiburg. He wrote the following about his break up with professor Heinkel: "That gentleman could be looked at as an idol only by those who do not know him well. I would not trade my little, but fundamental knowledge with his. He makes a secret of the most common processes that are described in almost every chemistry textbook, and one has to pull them out of him with a rope. At the same time he scorns all prudent philosophy. Once, when I started speaking about a chemical process, he ordered me to keep silent immediately, because it was not done according to his hypothetical concept, but on the basis of mechanical and hydrostatics principles. He made fun of my explanations, calling them nonsense." Lomonosov's hot-tempered and passionate nature could not be subdued to a dull system of teaching.

He left Freiburg earlier than he should have, but nonetheless, professor Heinkel recognized that Mikhailo completed the academic program. In his letter to the St. Petersburg Academy of Science he said the following: "I must admit that, in my view, Mr. Lomonosov, who successfully completed a course of theoretical and metallurgical chemistry, as well as the marksscheider (mining- M. A.) in art, soil, stones, salts, and waters, is thoroughly capable of teaching mechanics, in which he is very well informed."

Apart from his scientific research, Lomonosov became a very good poet. In honor of the victory of the Russian army over the Turks, he even wrote the following ode:

Overtake of Khotin

Not daring to fall into combat again
The foe is fleeing through empty gaps,
Forgetful of sword, camp, and the disgrace
He bears. In scary displays of blood
His perished friends are lying,
And the weightless trembling of nimble leaves
Terrifies, like the whistle of heavy shells,
flying fast like the breeze.

The verses, written in the new poetic style of iamb, were a sensation in Petersburg. The young man became a famous poet overnight. Belinskyi later noted that Russian literature began when Lomonosov sent abroad his ode devoted to the

Overtake of Khotin. While his glory at home was growing, the author made his way back to Marburg. There he hoped to obtain a permission to return home. Unexpectedly, his wandering in the foreign country lasted a bit longer.

Lomonosov's stout and strong figure attracted the attention of a Prussian officer who was recruiting soldiers into the army. The officer invited the hungry student for dinner, and the next morning he woke up with a tie that was worn by the Prussian soldiers, and a few coins in his pocket. He had become a royal hussar. Together with the other new recruits, Mikhailo was taken to a fort. It took him some time before he could flee. When he finally reached Marburg, he obtained his permission to return home.

Mikhailo had to leave his young wife with her mother. He planned to bring her to Petersburg when circumstances would allow him to do so. Later he did just that.

To Find the Accord of Reasons

In June of 1741, after 5 years of studying in Germany, Lomonosov returned to Russia. He was 30, and he was strong and full of new ideas. This was the beginning of his intensive and diverse work at the Saint Petersburg Academy.

Lomonosov's versatile talents, combined with his incredible capacity for work and diligence, produced fantastic results. He tried to understand the laws of nature, in order to reveal the general "accord of reason." He founded and developed a new school for the atomic and molecular composition of substances, and on its basis he discovered the nature of heat and cold, overthrowing the then universally accepted theory of "thermogen". The Russian scientist was the first to give a clear formulation of the law of preservation of substance and motion.

According to Mikhailo, there existed a close link between physics and chemistry. Apart from chemical experiments, he also made "optical, magnetic, and electric experiments, with various substances." Such observations enabled him to better understand the concealed science of nature, and Lomonosov created a new science on their basis - physical chemistry. The scientific world didn't understand and accept the new science until the 19th century.

Lomonosov made a whole series of discoveries in physics, chemistry, optics, crystallography, geology, meteorology, and astronomy. He discovered the existence of an atmosphere on Venus, and laid the foundation for astrophysics as a science. In his work, Lomonosov summarized and developed technologies for the production of various metals. He always insisted that the final objective of the development of theoretical problems should be their practical implementation.

Mikhailo also constructed many new instruments and tools. For example, he was the first to suggest the idea of making a telescope without a flat reflecting mirror. He constructed a special night telescope in order to allow seamen sailing in the northern seas to see approaching icebergs. For measuring the direction and strength of the wind, Lomonosov constructed an anemometer. In addition, the outstanding inventor amazed the scientific world with his instrument for measuring the gravitational force of celestial planets on the earth. He also developed ideas for a solar oven, periscope, and refractometer.

Open Starry Heaven

Lomonosov did a lot for Russia. He created the first chemical laboratory in Russia, organized an expedition for the development of the Northern sea, and working for the establishment of the first Russian atlas.

Gertzen said that Lomonosov was "eager to learn everything, and would take one subject after the other and understand it fully."

Mikhailo Lomonosov put many of his scientific and philosophical observations into verses of great majesty. Inspired by the extraordinary shining sky over Saint Petersburg, he wrote his *Evening Reflections*. In these he discusses the reasons for the unusual natural phenomenon.

Day has hidden its whitish face;
Dusky night has fallen down;
Inky shadows have climbed the hills;
All the sunbeams are gone
The heaven is open, full of stars
Like countless lights, in abyss after abyss
What are the laws of nature?
Daybreak comes from twilight fields!
Is this the place the sun inhabits?

How could a frozen hazy vapor
Conceive a blazing spark in frost?

Lomonosov was impressed with the mosaics brought from Rome by count Vorontsov, and developed an interest in them. Into every subject he brought his scientific methods and his creative inspiration. The scientist used the latest discoveries in chemistry to develop a technology for creating colored glass. He made over 3,000 experiments, and came up with a few discoveries. Antique mosaics held no secret from him. Using new technologies, Lomonosov created 40 panels of mosaics.

His small portrait of Peter I, which was offered to the senate, can be seen today in the Hermitage. Specialists agree that this is one of the best portraits of the reformist Tsar. Seven artists worked under Lomonosov to achieve the Poltava Battle, made of 900,000 pieces of tainted glass. The piece was intended for the Petropavlovsk Church. Today it decorates the walls of the Academy of Science of Saint Petersburg. Lomonosov was elected honorary member of the Bologna Academy of Science for his work in the field of mosaics, in 1764. Italian newspapers published enthusiastic articles about Lomonosov's discoveries in the field of colored glass, and also about his own masterpieces.

Literature was part of Lomonosov's scientific and artistic work. His odes, poems, tragedies and epigrams, were famous, and not only in Russia. His *Russian Grammar,* written in 1755, became the most popular textbook. Until the mid 19th century, generations of Russians learned the basics of grammar with this book. It was reprinted 11 times, and translated into German, French and Greek. Lomonosov himself wrote, "Charles I, the Roman Emperor, said that Spanish is used to speak with the Gods, French with friends, German with enemies... Italian with women. Yet if he knew the Russian language, he would use it to communicate with all. For the Russian language contains the majesty of the Spanish language, the life of the French language, the strength of the German language, the smoothness of the Italian language, and on top of that, the rich and condensed expressions of the Latin and Greek languages...the rhetoric art of Cicero, the elegance of Virgil, and the poetry of Ovidus do not lose anything in Russian...".

In 1748 Lomonosov became a member of the Historical Society, which was part of the Academy. His responsibilities included the analysis of all works on the history of Russia. Soon he was in conflict with the official historiographer of the Russian State, Miller. They had radically opposed views on Russian history. In his dissertation, Miller developed the Norman theory of the origin of the Russian nation. In his efforts to defend the honor of the Russian nation, Lomonosov managed to have Miller's work declared unsuitable, and dangerous - imposing its destruction. In 1751 he started gathering materials for a new history of Russia.

The Empress Elizabeth expressed her wish to see this work as soon as possible. That is probably why her assistant Ivan Shuvalov encouraged Lomonosov to put aside the "unnecessary" subjects of chemistry and physics, and focus all of his energy on preparing to write the history of Russia and Russian literature. The scientist's answer was slightly sarcastic, "As far as my works in physics and chemistry are concerned, there is no need to abandon them, and I could not possibly do it. Every person needs to rest from work, and I will rest from the work of gathering and writing the history of Russia and Russian literature, for a few hours a day, by conducting physical and chemical experiments - instead of playing pool - as my experiments replace entertainment just like movement can replace medical drugs, and on top of that, they can be useful for our Motherland." This work of many years ended in 1760, with the publication of *A Short Russian Chronicle of Genealogy*. The book told the stories of the first Russian knights and Czars, including Peter I. Its first part, entitled *Ancient Russian History From the Beginning of the Russian Nation to the End of Knight Yaroslav I, i.e. to 1054,* was printed in 1766, after the death of Lomonosov.

Administrative work at the Saint Petersburg Academy, where Lomonosov had served as a leading official since 1757, required a lot of work. For many years the Germans were leading the Academy, and blocking the progress of Russian science and education. Lomonosov considered that to be a tragedy, as he was convinced that only education could increase the strength of a people, and consequently, a nation. For this reason, Lomonosov proposed a reorganization of the Academy, and started fighting the conservative party. Lomonosov was in charge of the Geographic Department of the Academy's school and university, which enabled him to found a new system for future Russian specialists. He worked out an integrated system of three degrees: school, university, and academy. The school provided a basic education to prepare students for the university. Lomonosov also paid attention to the needs of students. He created dormitories, made sure scholarships were paid on time, and made sure that outstanding students were financially supported. He insisted on the importance of science for Russia, stressing its role in the life of society.

Science feeds the youngster's mind,
And gives joy to adults,
Adds delight to a cheerful moment,
And brightens up sadness
It's an escape from daily anguish,
And not at all burdensome
It can be carried everywhere
In city noise, and in desert,
Among people, and in lonely quiet
The study and the work are sweet...

Never forgetting his hard road to science, Lomonosov managed to organize the opening of Moscow University for all social classes. He prepared the charter for the university, and moreover, convinced the Empress' protege Count Shuvalov of the importance of the project. The charter which launched Moscow Academy was signed on January 12, 1755, on Tatiana Day. Lomonosov was not even invited to the opening ceremony. For us, the university is forever connected to the greatest scientists, and for more than two centuries Tatiana Day has been celebrated as the founding date of Moscow University, and Student's Day.

A Hero of Science

Lomonosov's contribution to science is celebrated in Russia and abroad. In 1760, he was elected an honorary member of the Swedish Academy of Sciences. As a result, he wrote and sent to the Swedish Academy his scientific work, *Thoughts on the origin of ice mountains in northern seas*, in which he classified different types of ice and explained the origin of icebergs. In Russia, Lomonosov was decorated by Empress Elizabeth "for outstanding mastery of arts," and Catherine II paid him a private visit. Recognizing his artistic work, the Academy of Arts elected Lomonosov an honorary member.

Lomonosov' activities were often burdened with a struggle against conservative professors. His discoveries contradicted traditional teachings and were laughed at. His works, aimed at improving the situation of his Motherland, were long ignored by leaders. He died at the age of 54. His body, though strong since childhood, couldn't cope with a bad cold. What destroyed the health of this strong hero? The years of privations during his studies? Twenty five years of unconditional work? Maybe he was just tired of fighting untalented people. Before his death, Lomonosov told his colleague Shteling, "My friend, I see I have to die, and I look at death with peace and calm; my only regret is that I couldn't achieve everything I started for the benefit of my Motherland, for the expansion of science and the glory of the Academy, and now, at the end of my life, I have to admit that my efforts will disappear with me".

Lomonosov's concern was grounded. The scientist was too far ahead of his time, and his conservative contemporaries couldn't accept his discoveries. The famous physicist Sergey Ivanovich Vavilov wrote about Lomonosov, "Only now, two centuries later, can we understand fully, and value all the work accomplished by this extraordinary scientist. The work he accomplished in the fields of physics, chemistry, astronomy, machine engineering, geology, geography, linguistics, and history, is worthy of the activities of an entire academy."

JEAN LE ROND D'ALEMBERT

(1717 - 1783)

He was not only a prominent mathematician, physicist, and practicing astronomer, but a famous philosopher, literary scientist, and educator, as well as one of the authors of the famous French encyclopedia.

A Foundling

On a chilly November night in 1717, a policeman who was making a watch round near St. Jean-Le-Rond church heard the barely audible cry of a baby. He went to the place where the disturbing sound was coming from, and found a baby boy on the steps of a church.

The foundling was delivered to the police station. He was so weak that the police commissar felt sorry for him, and did not send him to an orphanage. The boy was also wrapped in an expensive blanket, and this indicated that he might have some relatives who would pay for his upbringing. Fortunately, a nurse was found in a nearby village who agreed to take the boy for some time.

This was how the life of the future great French scientist was saved. He turned out to be the illegitimate child of French Artillery General Destouches. The child's eccentric mother, a writer name Madame de Tencin, decided to get rid of the unwanted child while the general was away. When he was back in Paris he made inquiries, and found his son. He took his son away from the village, and found him a place in a family of glaziers by the name of Rousseau. The kindhearted Madame Rousseau felt sorry for the general, and for the abandoned child, and agreed to adopt him. The child was barely alive, but Madame Rousseau promised the grieving general that she would do everything possible to nurse him to health, and raise him well. At his baptism the boy was named Jean Baptiste Le Rond, after the name of the church where he was found. When the boy grew up he called himself Jean Le Rond D'Alembert.

General Destouches frequently visited the boy at the Rousseau's, and spared no means for his education and upbringing. He was delighted by the child's playfulness and inquisitiveness, and was amazed by the answers, given by the five year old boy, on various questions. He saw in the boys answers, an indication of an extraordinary mind. Soon he sent his boy to a school where the teachers also noted his various gifts, and shared in the father's delight.

The Rousseau family treated the boy as their own child, and the kindhearted Madame Rousseau loved Jean even better than her own children. Jean Le Rond lived in an amicable family among simple and sincere people. Yet Destouches' sensitive and kind heart could not accept that the boy was deprived of his mother's love.

Madame de Tencin was a talented writer and a charming woman. She had a reputation for being the acclaimed hostess of a well-known salon that was attended by writers, artists, and high-ranking dignitaries. According to her contemporaries, while she had personal charm and gentleness, she was also heartless and seductive. She called the guests of her salon "my zoo" and wrote that her profession of writing was "the most miserable occupation." She continued, "Every shoemaker can be sure that his work will be sold, while a writer can never be sure about his book, no matter how good it is."

Undoubtedly Madame de Tencin was very clever, witty and attractive. Her left-to-the-mercy-of-fate son certainly inherited some of her talents, but one could only imagine what his morals would have been, had he been brought up by a mother like Madame de Tencin. Maybe fate deprived him of his mother's influence on purpose, in order to protect his bright mind.

The relationship between Madame de Tencin and General Destouches was just a troublesome episode, but the determined soldier refused to submit himself to her indifference. Sometimes he visited his old mistress and the mother of his only child, and told her about their talented son. Once he got her so intrigued that the "high society lioness" decided to descend from her sky heights to visit the boy.

At that time Jean was seven years old. Destouches, patting his son on the head with his bearish hand, exclaimed, "Isn't it a pity, Madame, that such a lovely and talented boy has been mercilessly thrown to the mercy of fate?" It is hard to say what Madame de Tencin felt when she saw her son, but Jean's first encounter with his mother was also his last one. She just said, leaving the room, "It is stuffy here."

At the age of ten, Jean lost his father too. Shortly before his death, Destouches asked his relatives to look after his unfortunate Jean, and they did not refuse.

At the age of thirteen, Jean Le Rond entered the Mazarin College. During his three years of study at this elite school, the boy greatly impressed his teachers. He studied rhetoric, literature, physics, and mathematics. He knew the Latin and Greek languages well, and could read Archimedes and Ptolemes in their original form. The school system at that time paid great attention to effective public speaking, and D'Alembert finished his schooling as an excellent orator. The young man easily passed all of his examinations and received his Bachelor of Arts degree. Then he attended the Legal Academy for two years and became a doctor of law. According to professors, Jean could be successful at any initiative. His clear mind and eloquence promised him a brilliant career as a lawyer, but D'Alembert did not want this for himself. Defending criminals was against his conscience, and after all, the innocent among the accused were few.

Jean's adoptive parents were proud of their son. They dreamed of a prosperous future for him, and a high social standing. In this regard, the occupation of physician seemed to them to be the most attractive profession for him. Jean's family persistently tried to persuade him to study medicine, but his heart was elsewhere.

Above all, Jean valued and loved mathematics. Jean's first mathematics teacher, Carone, managed to implant in the boy's heart a love for the "queen of science." The Rousseau family was seriously concerned with Jean's interest in math, as they thought mathematics was an incomprehensible, impractical, and absolutely unpromising science. Out of respect for the opinion of his parents, and in order not to bother them, he took his math textbooks to his friend Diderot's house. Quite sincerely, he promised that he would make an effort to become a doctor of medicine.

But alas, his sincere, passionate, and impatient nature could not overcome itself. The young mathematician stayed in the library for longer and longer hours, spending days and nights pouring over algebraic books. Gradually, under various excuses, he carried all of his mathematics books back home. He became entirely taken with mathematics.

"Mathematics - my old and loyal love...."

said Jean Le Rond D'Alembert when he became an acknowledged scientist. He enjoyed mathematics greatly, and had an immensely wide spectrum of interests.

Jean's hard work brought impressive results. His research on the theory of partial differential equations played a fundamental role in the further development of mathematics, as did his immense contributions to the theory of complex variables. The widely practiced principle of convergence of series carries the name of D'Alembert. Jean also studied the problems of string oscillation, and successfully solved the general wave equation. This work, along with works of Euler and Bernoulli, laid the foundation for physical mathematics. Other famous scholars, like Lagrange and Herman, were working in the same direction, at the same time as Jean Le Rond.

Jean Le Rond D'Alembert was a mathematician, but his inquisitive mind penetrated every area he turned his eyes to. He worked in celestial mechanics, and successfully explained the mathematical theory behind Newton's discovery of the precession of the equinoxes and the perturbation in the orbits of the planets.

In one of his astronomic works, Lagrange tried to analytically establish the curved path of Venus, using the curve of sun. He was criticized for using numerical methods traditionally used by astronomers. Le Rond's statement in connection to this criticism became widely known. "One should not behave like a fairy tale hero who prays to Jupiter and Hercules to get rid of fleas," he said.

An instructive statement, and not only for scholars.

A strict mathematical approach was the basis for many of Jean Le Rond's discoveries. In *Insight into the General Cause of Winds*, Le Rond proves the existence of air ebbs and ocean ebbs. As a result, for more than two hundred years, the name of D'Alembert name has been well known to meteorologists all over the world. The same strict mathematical approach enabled Jean Le Rond to study the dynamics of solid bodies, and solve the problem of nutation - oscillatory movements of rotating solid bodies. Students of universities and technical schools throughout the whole world study differential equations whose solutions were given by the genius mathematician, Jean le Rond, but it was the principle of D'Alembert that made him world famous.

D'Alembert Principle

In 1740, in his *Discourse on Dynamics,* Jean le Rond formulated a principle that became one of the main rules applied in dynamics. It was later named the D'Alembert principle, after him. He was only 26 years old, and this discovery immediately made him famous. There were many scientists who had tried to find new methods of solution for this problem of dynamic mechanics, but none of them had succeeded. D'Alembert's principle brought problems of dynamics to the dimension of statics. The essence of D'Alembert's principle was: "If all forces acting on the system or mechanism cause inertia, then the system will be steady, i.e. statically definite."

Lagrange wrote the following about the conclusion drawn by D'Alembert: "It suggests a direct and general method for solving, or at least presenting in the form of equations, all problems of mechanic dynamics that could ever be imagined."

What else could be added to this acknowledgment, made by the founder of analytical mechanics? In plain words, Jean Le Rond was one of the most prominent scientists of the 18th century.

One Out of Forty Immortals

Jean Le Rond D'Alembert was also a philosopher, an art historian, and a man of letters, in the golden age of the French Enlightenment. For his literary achievements, D'Alembert was elected at the age of 23 to the French Academy. He became one of forty immortals, as academicians were called in France.

Jealous Paris wits were saying that D'Alembert was a great writer among scientists, and a great scientist in literature, but this criticism was nothing more than a joke. Jean Le Rond was famous because his verse writing was exquisite and original. In one of his letters to Jean Le Rond, Voltaire wrote, "You are the only writer who says no more or less than what he wants to say. I consider you to be the best writer of this century."

Another contemporary writer, Lagarpe, considered Jean Le Rond to be one of the five most outstanding writers of France, along with Fontenelle, Buffon, Montesquieu, and Condillac. Jean Le Rond's real mother, the salon writer, never even dreamed of such fame.

Jean never thought of his fame. He was not vain, and had modest financial requirements that ensured him the serenity and freedom that only well off people have. He used this freedom to study and write about subjects besides mathematics. Le Rond was very clever in music, and he published a work called *On Freedom of Music*. He also wrote the biographies of many fellows at the Paris Academy.

Jean Le Rond's whole life was filled with tireless work. Madame Rousseau called her beloved son a philosopher, according to her own understanding of this word. For her, a common city dweller, the philosophers were strange people who worked like slaves the whole day and had nothing in life. Jean did not argue with her. He calmly listened with his usual slightly sarcastic expression. It was not because he agreed with everything she said that he did not argue with her. It was just because he was not in the habit of imposing his own views. Jean realized that absolute truth existed only in precise sciences, so all other expressions of life seemed to him to be relative or conditional. He believed that everyone was free to express any view they wanted.

Jean Le Rond was not seriously concerned about his fame, but he was a real philosopher. He seriously worked on the philosophic aspects of natural science. His work *Elements of Philosophy*, published in 1759, was well known. The scientist's most important belief was that people should not waste time. To him, everything else was unimportant when compared to his work.

Jean Le Rond D'Alembert became the most famous scholar of the Age of Enlightenment. He was given many honorable and high titles while he was alive, but the one that was most precious to him was always the title of "one out of forty immortals".

Encyclopedist

The whole of Europe took into consideration the opinion of scientists, but the title of encyclopedist was not only given to D'Alembert because of his versatility. Jointly, with Denis Diderot, Jean became the imagination behind, and the coauthor of an impressive project: the publication of the grandiose seventeen-volume *Encyclopedia on Science, Arts, and Craftsmanship*. The emergence of this reference book became an important event for France, and for the whole of Europe.

A group of French educators joined their efforts to create this publication, in order to challenge the basis of the Old World. Undoubtedly, the main goal of these talented people was none other than to turn France into the most educated nation in the world, and to advance the development of an entire civilization! The educators believed that the proliferation of education, and its practical application for a more prudent public organization, would enable humankind to solve all social, political, technical and even moral problems. This sounds a bit naive, but undoubtedly the Encyclopedia profoundly influenced the situation in France. It shook the foundations of the feudal society, and prepared it ideologically for the Great French Revolution.

The scientists and writers who participated in the preparation of the Encyclopedia, and became known as encyclopedists, were Voltaire, Jean-Jacques Rousseau, Montesquieu, P. Golbach and others. D'Alembert wrote a foreword for the encyclopedia called *Essay on the Origins and the Development of Sciences*. The foreword was an overview of human knowledge in its entirety at the time, and it marked the beginning of a new epoch in the intellectual life of France, and the whole world. One of his contemporaries made the following statements about the article, "Future generations, when reading this article, will understand that all sciences can be mastered by a human; D'Alembert is a remarkable writer, a great mathematician, and an outstanding philosopher. At the same time, he can harmonically combine the beauty, ability and power of words, making his creative works especially captivating." Apart from the introduction, D'Alembert authored all parts concerning mathematics and physics, including the articles called *Differentials, Equations, Geometry,* and *Dynamics*. Clearly D'Alembert had a prominent role in the publication of the most important French book of the 18th century. In the article on college, D'Alembert stood against the education system founded by the Jesuits, and suggested a new program of learning. In the article on Copernicus, he described the fight of the Inquisition against the heliocentric concept.

In the freedom-loving spirit of the French encyclopedia, sarcastic remarks directed at pseudo-scientists, arrogant noblemen, and hypocritical clergymen were not left unattended. The encyclopedia caused a social storm, and left nobody indifferent; people were either passionate supporters, or furious opponents. Society was taken with both admiration and hatred. The encyclopedists had to enter endless disputes, and deal with much persecution. Threats and slander were widely cast. The vanguard of this campaign consisted of "miserable connoisseurs" - a group of aggressive pseudo-scientists who always vehemently opposed every new and progressive idea.

"The great talents always invoke hatred, as iron gets eaten by rust. Only mediocrity has no enemy," wrote D'Alembert bitterly. He was a proud and very sensitive person. His sincere and extremely receptive heart was outraged by slander. He obviously was not created for a struggle against pseudo-patriots and jerks. Absorbed in his scientific research, he did not wish to waste his strength in a useless battle against mediocrity.

Le Rond found great enjoyment in his work. In a letter to Lagrange he said the following about his undertaking in science: "I am not in a habit of being continuously involved in work on one and the same subject. I leave it for some time just to come back to it when I wish to. Such a manner does not harm my success." It was this quality that enabled D'Alembert to become one of the authors of the greatest memorial to human thought in the 18th century, *Encyclopedia on Science, Arts and Craftsmanship*.

The title of "encyclopedist," given to him by his successors, serves Jean Le Rond D'Alembert best.

Openness and sincerity were the main qualities of Le Rond. He could forgive everything but charlatanism in science. He also hated cupidity and greed. Le Rond was a member of many academies of science, but he sustained a miserable salary. All his honorary titles did not earn him any means. It seemed as though everyone forgot about the need to support the famous scientist.

He did, however, acquire an enormous influence in the scientific world, and he used it to support young talents.

D'Alembert had a very sophisticated mind, but simple feelings. He had a compassionate personality, and was always eager to help. He used to say that he didn't like excess, and did not think that he needed to have something excessive when other people were deprived of the most basic things, and these were not just empty words; he lived by them. Le Rond supported his adoptive parents, taught lessons for his first math teacher, helped students, and mentored young scholars.

Once when young Laplace, the son of a poor Norman peasant, came to him with a recommendation letter from an important person, D'Alembert refused to meet him. When Laplace wrote a letter to him in which he laid out his views on mechanics, D'Alembert answered him the next day. "You have recommended yourself and that's enough for me," he said.

This answer characterizes D'Alembert very precisely. Soon after the meeting with D'Alembert, Laplace was given a position as a mathematics teacher at the military school where Napoleon had studied. Later, Laplace became the Minister of Internal Affairs in the cabinet of the first Council of France.

Thanks to the friendly disposition of a Prussian King, Frederic the Great, D'Alembert also managed to help his fellow scientists. He asked for an increase in the pension to the great Euler, who was burdened by a large family and was thinking of leaving Prussia for Russia. He also recommended the prominent French scientist Lagrange to a Berlin academy. Frederic highly respected D'Alembert, and on more than one occasion he offered him the position of President of the Berlin Academy of Science. No matter how flattering and financially attractive this offer was, D'Alembert gracefully refused. He passionately loved to be independent, and one of his friends fairly called him a "slave of freedom." He explained his last refusal of Frederic's offer with the following words: "Since my early childhood deprivations taught me to be satisfied with little, and I am ready to share what I have with people who are poorer than me. Loneliness and the poor life absolutely correspond to my character - my passionate desire for independence, and my wish to avoid people and society... I owe nothing to the government of France; from them I can expect only harm in the future and nothing good; however, I do have obligations to my country. The latter has been generous to me, acknowledging my achievements, and rewarding me for my sufferings. On my part it would be immensely ungrateful to leave such a country."

D'Alembert's refusal upset the Prussian Emperor, but Frederic the Great's respect for the scientist only increased. He informed Le Rond that he had granted him an appropriate pension. Frederic wrote to Louis XV that since the means of subsistence for a French scientist were much lower than his achievement, he was obliged to correct the mistake. Later, thanks to the persistence of Minister Larganson, the wounded French King allocated a pension to D'Alembert. Contemporaries said about Larganson, "He likes educated people and doesn't envy them because he is a clever person." This is a brilliant statement. Generosity is an indication of cleverness.

Catherine II also highly respected D'Alembert. She persistently invited him to come to Saint Petersburg, together with his friends, and offered him a fantastic salary for educating the heir of the Russian throne, Paul I. Jean Le Rond D'Alembert also refused this invitation. His reason for this refusal was his ignorance about life in Russia, and most importantly, the responsibility placed on the educator of the heir to the Russian throne. Catherine II was disappointed by Le Rond's refusal, but she expressed her respect for the great and famous thinker by giving him a pension from the Saint Petersburg academy of science that was twice the size of the pension given by Frederic.

D'Alembert avoided golden cages, and science was his life. He greatly esteemed France, and especially Paris. He couldn't live even a week away from the city. The great scientist was tied to Paris by a great and hopeless love, Mademoiselle de Lespinasse. She was also an illegitimate child of a noble lady, Madame Daliban. The legal inheritors hated the girl, and right after her mother's death they disinherited her from her share of legacy. D'Alembert saw her for the first time at the house she shared with his friend, Madame du Deffand. Julie de Lespinasse was a proud, unusually talented, and clever girl, though her heart had been hurt by her unfair life. The clever and educated girl soon outperformed her hostess, and became the princess of the salon. Madame du Deffand could not be happy about this, as the salon was the meaning of her life, but when Madame Lespinasse left the house, the salon became empty. The young girl soon opened her own salon, and it became the most fashionable salon in Paris.

First D'Alembert and Madame de Lespinasse were linked by friendship. Both of them were clever in philosophy and literature. All of their friends were delighted by their friendship - even Voltaire - but Julie de Lespinasse's interest in the young, talented man tormented her friend. Jean looked at her like at an ill child. Madame de Lespinasse struggled with herself, and love and passion exhausted her strength. She died in D'Alembert's arms. What kept D'Alembert tied to Madame de Lespinasse? Maybe her similarity with his mother?

When Jean's beloved one died, a light extinguished in his sorrowful eyes, and life seemed to lose its value. If it had not been for mathematics he might have followed his beloved to the grave. However, time cures all ills, and Jean's sorrow was no exception.

At the height of his years, Le Rond said, "A really fair

person should prefer his family over himself, his country over his family, and humankind over his country."

Jean Le Rond D'Alembert died in solitude on an October night in 1783. He was a brilliant scientist, an outstanding personality, and a clever philosopher, who left a great scientific and spiritual legacy to human kind.

MICHAEL FARADEI
(1791 - 1876)

A bookbinder, laboratory assistant, and self-made man, he spent forty years working on electromagnetic phenomenon, and founded a new area of study in electromagnetic fields. The advent of the "era of electricity" was to a large extent anticipated by Faradei's discoveries.

Self-Taught

Michael Faradei was born to the family of a London blacksmith, James Faradei, on September 22, 1791. He was the third and youngest child in an amicable, religious family. Work was the basis of family upbringing.

At that time England was experiencing an industrial boom, and the family of such a fine professional as Michael's father could have lived comfortably, had the hard work not wrecked his health. The family's modest means did not allow them to give the children a serious education. There were no state owned schools at that time in England, and Michael only finished primary school, where he learned how to read, write, and count. The future great physicist did not study algebra or geometry. It seems incredible, but Faradei learned all of his immense knowledge only thanks to his own persistence, industriousness, and bright mind.

At the age of thirteen, Michael started his working life. He was not born with a powerful physique, so his parents sent him to be an apprentice at the book bindery under a book store. One can presume that this decision determined Faradei's destiny. At the bindery, the young man could read the books that needed to be binded. The bookstore was also a sort of a cultural center, attended by the area's local book fans.

Faradei's inquisitive mind was always absorbing new things. He read much, and with a great interest, but he did not read the fiction and adventure books most of his contemporaries read. Rather, he preferred to read the Britannica. He was especially interested in everything concerning electricity.

Once he found a popular book called *Conversations on Chemistry*, written by the wife of a local physician, Mrs. Marse. He could not help personally performing the chemical experiments depicted in the book. The results of this first scientific research amazed the young man and awakened him as an experimenter. Later Faradei confessed that it was this book which opened to his "young, unlearned and curious mind, the laws of a boundless world of natural science." He considered Mrs. Marse to be his first teacher, and remained grateful to her for all of his life. Later he would send her his writings.

This feeling of gratitude toward everyone who helped him find his path, never abandoned Faradei. He valued and appreciated his family's understanding and support, as well as the modest shillings that they gave him for buying the materials needed for experiments. By saving his own money, the young man was able to buy chemical substances, and at night after he got home from work, he conducted experiments at home. He made an electric static machine out of a bottle. Out of a zinc tea cup and a few copper pennies, he made a galvanic battery, and learned about the electrolysis of salts and acids.

At that time, new sciences were becoming popular in the dynamically developing England. Various researchers in many fields would read lectures for the public on Saturday and Sunday nights at the London Royal Institute. Faradei eagerly took advantage of this source of knowledge. He went to lectures on Chemistry, Physics, and Natural Philosophy, and attended private classes to become knowledgable in literature. He also started drawing.

Faradei met interesting and intelligent young men at the Philosophic Society, and his communication with them expanded his horizons. In those years Faradei always felt that he lacked knowledge, and spent all of his free time educating himself. He was profoundly impressed by the public lectures of the famous chemist, Hamphrey Davi. Davi's lectures influenced Faradei greatly, making him dream of doing his own scientific work, but achieving this dream seemed impossible. His work at a new book bindery did not leave any time for self education. The young man grew disappointed, feeling that his dreams were doomed. He decided to write to the great Davi about his passionate desire to do science. He attached to the letter the carefully written and bound lectures of Davi.

Of course Davi noted the diligence and persistence of the young man, and the young binder's naivete and enthusiasm probably summoned the famous chemist's condescending smile. However, soon after reading the letter an accident happened during an experiment: Davi injured his eyes and temporarily lost the ability to read and write. This accident determined Faradei's destiny. Davi remembered the motivated young man and invited him to be his personal secretary for some time.

Davi was pleasantly surprised by the young man's extensive knowledge, and decided to help him enter the university. Fortune was favoring the self-taught book binder. In 1813, on Davi's recommendation, Faradei was accepted as an assistant at the chemical laboratory of the Royal Institute.

Do Eggs Teach Chickens?

At first he washed test tubes and looked after the laboratory, supervised by Davi. Then he was entrusted with preparing test tubes for experiments and demonstrations, and later, with assisting Davi during lectures. Finally, Faradei's dream came true, and he started participating in research work. He was happy because he was finally free to indulge his passion.

Soon Davi and his wife decided to go on a voyage to Europe, and since their house maid could not accompany them,

Faradei was offered a temporary position as their chamberlain. However resistant Faradei's pride was to this suggestion, he reluctantly agreed. For him, the son of a blacksmith from a London suburb, it was the only way he would have the fantastic opportunity of seeing Europe's culture and science. He would have been completely content with the arrangement if it had not been for one detail; the obligations of a valet under Davi's bossy and capricious wife were very hard on Faradei. She took every opportunity to humiliate the young man. On more than one occasion Michael thought of returning back to England. Only his desire for education kept him from doing so.

On a tour with Davi Michael, Faradei had the opportunity to meet with celebrities of European science. The French and Italian chemists had an appreciation for the talent of beginner scientists, and thanks to his intelligence, good-nature, and modesty, Faradei quickly found sympathetic people. He met many valuable and devoted friends on that trip.

When he got back to England Faradei was promoted from an assistant to a full fledged researcher. He was given the right to conduct independent research, and he did so without delay. Soon the scientific journal of the Royal Society published Faradei's first scientific work. Since 1816 the young scientist had started writing his first set of lectures called, *Description of Properties of Substances, Types of Substances and Perception of Simple Bodies* at the Philosophic Society. As a chemist, he achieved much success in the research of liquefied gases. He also played an instrumental role in the discovery of the design of benzol.

Michael Faradei's success made him widely known in scientific circles. In 1824 his colleagues proposed that he be elected into the Royal Society. The only vote against Faradei's membership in the Royal Society, strange as it may be, belonged to his teacher Davi. Apparently he could not deal with the breathtaking scientific career of his former lab assistant, and demanded that Faradei be removed from the list of candidates. However, Davi's campaign did not have much success, and Faradei was elected a member of the highest scientific establishment of Great Britain.

Later Davi confessed that M. Faradei was his greatest discovery. As for Michael, he was far from petty human grudges, and as a person who valued science more than anything, he had high esteem for his teacher as a great chemist whom he would never forget, and whom he was obliged to.

The King of Physics

"It is easier to make nature speak than to solve its riddles," said Faradei in a fit of temper. Since 1821, Michael had been overtaken with the idea of comprehending the nature of electromagnetic phenomenon. He set out to accomplish the task of "transforming magnetism into electricity." The persistent scientist devoted more than ten years of his life to finding this solution.

"Faradei is of a medium height. Lively, and joyful, his eyes are always alert, and his motions are quick and confident. He is precise, neat, and devoted to his work. He lives in his laboratory among his test tubes and instruments. He goes there in the morning, and returns home late at night with the regularity of a merchant who spends the whole day at the office." That is what the French chemist Duma wrote about the rising star of English science.

In his first work on "electricity" Faradei created a laboratory model of a future electric engine. In the fall of 1831 he published a statement on the discovery of electromagnetic induction, which became the basis for modern electric engineering. This was a real breakthrough, and at forty years old, the scientist had immortalized his name forever. Soon after Faradei's discovery, the first electromagnetic generators of electricity were designed.

Faradei's research work is described in detail in his fundamental work, *Experimental Research in Electricity*. This book is a practical chronicle of Faradei's scientific triumphs, and a history of forty long years of research. From the epoch discovery of electromagnetic induction, and his hypotheses of the existence of electromagnetic waves, the author moves to establish similarity between various types of electricity and electrolysis. Then he investigates the phenomenon of self induction and electricity, and founds a theory on the existence of the electromagnetic field.

This scientist's titanic work opened up a new field of research. The scientific world at that time did not have the appropriate terminology to describe electromagnetic processes. Today these complex concepts and notions are described with a mathematical language: induction, vector, electric charge, inductive coefficient, etc. They were described by Faradei using words or figures. However, because he lacked the appropriate vocabulary to explain his discoveries, he was not always understood by his contemporaries. In 1840 the genius scientist proposed an idea about the unity and mutual transformation of various "natural forces." Faradei came very close to understanding the laws of preservation and transformation of energy, which were formulated a few years later by the German physicist Mayer. Faradei's contemporaries highly appreciated his scientific achievements, and he was elected a member of all the world academies. He also became a director of the laboratory of the Royal Institute.

Faradei loved his profession, and it seemed that he did not notice that the enormous overload caused by hard work was ruining his health. When Faradei understood that he was no longer able to combine his scientific and engineering research, he had to leave engineering. The circle of his interest was very broad, including engineering, physics, chemistry, biology, and the arts; all were interesting for the scientist's inquisitive mind. However, his disabilities forced him to pick the most important thing. The science of electricity was always the priority for Faradei.

The History of a Candle

Faradei never left his academic activities behind. He never forgot the significance of public lectures at the Royal Institute in his own life, so he started a practice of reading sets of Christmas lectures for children. For them, he read a series of lectures on chemistry, thermal energy, and electricity. His lectures were accompanied by interesting experiments and tests, and they were very popular. In 1861 Faradei published his famous book, *The History of a Candle*. It was composed of his Christmas lectures, and it became so widely known that it was translated into all European languages. This book is still a benchmark of scientific and popular reading for children. At that time, Faradei also published his articles about platinum, and an eclipse. In 1862 Faradei published his final printed work. It was on gas ovens. At the same time, he was working to prove the influence of a magnetic field on the spectrum of a light source placed between the two poles of a magnet. Alas, Faradei did not manage to perform this experiment with his typical brilliance.

Faradei's energy was quickly abandoning him. More and

more he noticed signs of memory deterioration. He would often conduct experiments he already done the previous week. Enduring physical, mental, and psychological strains will undermine the human organism, and soon the genius scientist could not work at all. Faradei's letter to his friend Shenbain is filled with a real sadness. "I am destroying my writings again and again," Faradei wrote, "I do not know if I still can write a logical line...I can no longer write."

Faradei's inability to do his favorite work oppressed him more than his physical symptoms. The British government presented the great scientist with a beautiful stone mansion where he, abruptly grown old, withdrew from everyone until his death. He did see anybody except John Tindall, his disciple and successor. Sometimes Faradei's weakened hand reached to his books, and he would again read his favorites, Shakespeare and Byron.

Faradei avoided high society even when he was healthy, and considered many receptions and gatherings to be useless wastes of time. However, he had a weakness for theater. He was always happy when he managed to go to a premiere, and often became feverishly excited as a result of being so involved with the characters.

He also liked watching sunrises and sunsets - especially from a deserted sea shore. He was more like a poet or an artist in his appreciation of these beautiful scenes, than a physicist, but then who said scientist's are cold and unfeeling? That is not true!

Until his last moment, Faradei met each new day with a childish smile, and was saddened by the sunset. However, On August 27, 1867, he did not have to be sad. He died before the sun went down.

The British bachelor of Cambridge University, James

Clark Maxwell, took up his mentor Faradei's banner shortly before his death. He published a book called *The Dynamic Theory of Field* in which he developed and mathematically processed Faradei's theory, creating an electromagnetic theory of life.

Einstein said the following about the King of Physics: "It is hard for us, who absorbed Faradei's ideas with a mother's milk, to comprehend their whole greatness." In order to conceive the idea of a field, according to the author of the theory of probability, one needed an extraordinary mind that could immediately look into the essence of a matter - a mind that never got stuck in formulas.

Faradei, who paved a path for human kind into the world of electricity, despised people who were arrogant - especially scientists. He understood that science would continue to live and develop, and even the death of a genius was not a great loss for it. No theory can be unshakable and eternal. "Our successors will look at us the way we look at our predecessors," he stated. It can't be said better.

The French academician and chemist Duma, who knew Faradei well, wrote: "His perfection was a result of his constant self observation and invariable spiritual firmness...In everything that relates to a science I never met a mind more free, more clear, and more courageous."

We owe many of the achievements of civilization to Faradei's work, his mind, and his talents.

SOFIA KOVALIEVSKAYA
(1850 - 1891)

The author of outstanding mathematical works which greatly impacted the development of mechanics, physics, and astronomy. The winner of the Borden Prize founded by the French Academy of Sciences, and the King Oscar II Prize (the Swedish Academy of Science). The first woman elected as a Corresponding Member of the Russian Academy of Sciences.

"A soul of fire and thoughts"

On an autumn morning in the Tver region, the majestic sound of bells was flying over freshly ploughed fields and the golden carpet of the forests.

It was October 1, 1868, and Vladimir Kovalievski and Sofia Corvin- Krukovska were celebrating their wedding in the village of Palibino. Vassili Vassilievich Corvin-Krukoski was standing in the middle of the wedding euphoria like a dark mountain. He was looking even darker than he usually did.

In fact, the retired general was in the worst possible mood. His favorite daughter, the charming 18 year-old Sofia, talented, and noble; the direct descendent of patron of the arts Hungarian King Corvin, and the granddaughter of the famous astronomer Schubert; the daughter who inherited an extraordinary mind unheard of for a woman, and who could have been shining in the courts of Europe - was getting married to a translator!

Immediately after the wedding ceremony, a coach took the young couple away to Saint Petersburg. If the newly weds had spent at least one more day in the village, their parents would have understood the goal of this strange marriage. Sofia's elder sister Anna Corvin-Krukovska was also shocked by the event, but for another reason. The wedding of her younger sister had taken place in order to free her mind.

Both Anna and Sofia were generously talented, and both were educated at home, but their spirits were very different. Anna was talented and promising, but she was a dreamer. She was not determined, and not concentrated on her studies. Since her childhood, she had been the queen of children's balls. More recently, she had begun trying to write, and had even befriended Dostoevsky himself!

Sofia was 7 year younger, and had always admired her older sister, hoping to imitate her, but her father wouldn't allow her to daydream. He was well educated himself, and had a passion for mathematics. He considered the traditional education given to his daughters by governesses to be insufficient. When Sofia turned 8, a new teacher appeared in the house, Iossif Ignatievich Malevich. He had mastered basic knowledge in all of the main subjects, and had followed the development of pedagogy. He was able to develop a love for study and work in both of the little girls. The walls of the children's room were covered with lessons on Ostrogradski's differential equations. (Sofia mastered those concepts that were familiar to her from childhood surprisingly quickly in college, and they at once found their own meaning in her thoughts.)

Meanwhile, mathematics wasn't yet Sophia's favorite subject. To her father's greatest joy, she took an interest in mathematics after mastering the basics of geometry and algebra. She was not only good at choosing difficult subjects to work on, but she tried to prove theorems by herself. During the 10 years she took lessons with professor Malevich, she mastered Burdon's algebra, which was part of the program at Paris Universities.

During her free time, like her daydreaming sister, Sofia wrote poetry. It was the only passion shared equally by the Corvin-Krukovski sisters. Possibly this was because their great grandmother on their father's side was a Gypsy! No wonder both sisters were dreaming of discovering the world! The older sister was swayed by strong emotions, but the younger one thought only of how to carry on her education. Since she had seen "the infinite dimensions of science," mathematics became her passion.

Unfortunately, in the 1860's the doors of Russian universities were still closed to women. Women determined to carry on their education took private lessons, inviting professors home, or they moved to Europe, where traditions involving women's education were more democratic and progressive. However, the Russian capital was going through great changes, which made conditions better for women. The idea of a universal education was circulating, and the idea of emancipation for women was slowly penetrating society. A growing number of men were in support of women's education, yet the position of the government remained unchanged: women need no education!

Anna was convinced that her parents would not allow her to study abroad. Her emotive mind came up with a romantic solution; she had to make a fake marriage to obtain the status of a married woman. Then, with or without her younger sister, Anna could achieve her dream, and escape to a place where she could feel free and equal. She looked for her "savior" among the noblemen.

Vladimir Kovalievski seemed to be the ideal candidate for the project. An educated man, at the age of 26 he was already famous as a translator and polyglot. The books he published in his modest publishing house were immediately sold out. Anna offered to marry Vladimir fictively, but Vladimir suddenly announced that he wanted to marry Sofia. Maybe the charm of the charming younger sister, nicknamed the sparrow, seduced the heart of the young man? Or maybe he was able to identify the rare mind and talent of the 18 year-old Sofia.

Sofia's parents were disappointed by her choice. Her fiance was not talented or rich. It was clearly a bad match. They could only explain the determination of their younger daughter as a passion - and therefore accepted it. Even her strict father didn't try to convince his beloved Sofia that it was a bad idea. The old general loved his daughter, and trusted her bright mind. He didn't want to be an obstacle to her happiness, so he agreed

This fake wedding was probably unnecessary. The loving father, modern and educated, would probably have understood Sofia's determination to be a scientist, and would have spared her this unplanned decision, but can one talk sense into the great granddaughter of King Corvin? Can one talk sense into the granddaughter of a gypsy?

After reaching Saint Petersburg they each took a separate apartment, but they soon became good friends. They had a lot in common. Both were seriously involved in science, and loved literature. Sofia admired Vladimir's phenomenal abilities, including his memory and his talent for languages. He would dictate his translations so fast that it was not possible to write them down. Friends who shared the secret of their "marriage" and who were meeting them at lectures and in theaters were astonished by the unusual couple. Kovalievski was not only involved in translations, but also in geology.

The young couple moved to Vienna, and later to Germany. Vladimir settled in Iena, and soon received his doctoral degree in geology, which brought him recognition and fame. Sofia was able to gain permission to attend lectures in mathematics and physics in Heidelberg, and one year later moved to Berlin. She wanted to achieve her dream with the help of the most talented mathematician of Europe, Karl Weierstrass. Even though she had the support of leading mathematicians, she did not get permission to attend classes. She was in despair; there was almost no chance for private lessons from

Weierstrasse. She knew that the scientist was so absorbed by his work that he would refuse anyone asking for private lessons, but she decided to try anyway. Overcoming her shyness she went to see the scientist. He welcomed the visitor out of politeness, and in order to get rid of her, he gave her several extremely difficult problems to solve - problems he was giving to his most talented students in mathematics. He was convinced he had gotten rid of the visitor, and was slightly surprised when she came back a week later with finished solutions. The great Weierstrasse couldn't hide his surprise; only a talented mathematician could have found these solutions! He looked closely at his visitor and recognized the intelligence and charm in her young face.

Karl Weierstrasse, a leading scientist - called the greatest mind of his time - changed his habits, and accepted the task of guiding the scientific work of the talented woman. He became a scientific support, and a close friend for Sofia. The original mind of the young woman inspired him to solve new, unexpected problems. University professors were saying jokingly that they were grateful to Sofia, for she had made the great professor come out of his shell. The old professor became a support and a sound critic for the talented Sophia, who submitted all of her work to him.

Their relationship continued, even after Sophia became a celebrity. Her first work, *Partial differential equations, Abelian integrals* established her talent. She proved that the rings around Saturn were not in the shape of an ellipse, as Laplace stated, but that of an oval. Proud of her first success, Sofia started researching differential equations linked to physics and mechanics. For her doctoral thesis she prepared a work named *About the theory of differential equations*. This work was highly praised by university scientists for its elegant solution, and they gave Kovalievskaya the title of a doctor of mathematical philosophy, and Master of Arts. It was soon discovered that a similar work was conducted earlier by Augustin Cochis. As a result, the theorem came to be called the "Cochis-Kovalievskaya theorem." It is known to many technical university students, and anyone who loves mathematics cannot help but admire the elegance and simplicity of the theorem.

Soon after receiving her doctorate, the young Sophia had to stop her studies. Together with Kovalievski, she fled to France during the terrible days of the Commune to save her sister and her lover. Anna had fallen in love with Jacquelart, one of the leaders of the Paris Commune. The defeat of the movement announced nothing good for their future, as they were all to be guillotined. Only the efforts of General Corvin-Krukovski were able to save Jacquelart from death, and Anna from becoming a widow.

The romantic example of her sister had an influence on Sofia, who was acknowledged in the scientific world but completely alone. She had just turned 25, and she was a charming, blossoming young woman! The death of her father was a terrible loss for Sofia; he had loved her like no one else. She was never close to her mother, and her sister was too involved in family duties. Sofia thought of herself as a useless orphan. Burdened by her scientific work, she felt the need to have a loyal man by her side, to support her genuinely. She was also frustrated with her situation. She had a real husband who was a scientist like her, and who genuinely loved, and understood her. Sofia decided to accept her affection for Vladimir as real love.

In Saint Petersburg they began to live together, and since science was not enough to support them, they got involved in business. The couple believed that money was a force that must serve society. They decided to set aside their scientific work, which gave meaning to their lives, for enough time to improve their financial situation. They were building real estate, and their success proved true in the beginning. When their only daughter, Sofia, was born, everybody predicted she would be a millionaire.

Suddenly all of their plans fell through. They were bankrupt. Kovalievski could not accept the crash because he had abandoned his passion for it. Sofia woke up from her dream. She had always wanted to go back to her work. "Everything is fine, we will start our work again!" she reassured her depressed husband. The failure excited her, giving her energy and strength. In the dust of the attic, she found her books and her damp manuscripts from Berlin. The paper was yellow, and the ink was pale, but the thoughts she'd expressed years before were still fresh and up to date. Within one night Sofia translated into German her article about Abelian functions, and the next day she read a brilliant report at a scientific congress. The scientific world of Saint Petersburg welcomed her with enthusiasm.

Full of energy, Sofia could not do things halfway, and once again she devoted herself completely to science. She saw salvation in mathematics, not only for her, but for her family, and she tried to convince her husband. He was getting more and more depressed and closed off. Sofia saw that their relationship was deteriorating, and he was showing signs of mental disturbance. The disease increased, and in the spring of 1883, Kovalievski committed suicide.

Sofia learned about the tragic end of her husband while she was in Paris, where she was trying to renew her studies after 6 years of interruption. She took it to heart, and accused herself of being responsible for it. Later, she wrote a book with Swedish writer Edgren-Lefler, in which she described a woman who got married without love, and was unable to prevent the death of her husband because of her lack of love. The shock of her husband's death affected Sofia's health. Weierstrasse's student, Mittag-Lefler, a professor from Helsinki, was making efforts to promote Kovalievskaya to professor of mathematics at Stockholm University. He was in despair when he saw Sofia doing embroidery. The owner of such a talented mind could not, according to him, waste her time doing such meaningless activities. However, Sofia only needed some time to rest and recover. Soon she finished a fundamental work on the fragmentation of light in crystals, and received the highest mark from professor Weierstrasse. He had no doubt that the talented student would take her place among the professors of Stockholm University, and indeed, the invitation from Stockholm came very soon.

After she gave her first lecture in German, Sofia was swimming in applause, flowers, and congratulations. Six months later she mastered Swedish, and in June 1884 she became a professor at Stockholm University. This was the best time of her career. Kovalievskaya was working as never before, and her Swedish colleagues jokingly named her Michelangelo - for her energy and talent.

Her work in those years brought her international fame. In late 1888 she received, in a special ceremony given by the French Academy, the Bordin Prize. This special prize was awarded only 10 times in a period of 50 years, and always for partial solutions. It had never been awarded for the full solution of a problem. In the 3 years before Kovalievskaya was awarded the prize, it had not been awarded to anyone. This made the victory of the 38 year-old scientist even more precious. Her work, focusing on the most difficult issues of mathematics, was of the greatest importance to mechanics, physics, and astronomy. Because Kovalievskaya's work was recognized as particularly difficult, the prize was raised from 3,000 to 5,000 francs. This was an extraordinary success for Kovalievskaya, which brought her eternal glory. Later, the Swedish Academy of Science awarded her the King Oskar II Prize, for her research in a similar field.

Sofia's success provoked great enthusiasm in Russia. For the first time, a Russian woman was recognized by top world scientists. She became a real role model for Russian women who were determined to receive a higher education. She received a terrific welcome in Russia. In November 1889, she was elected correspondent of the department of physics and mathematics at the Russian Academy of Science. On her visit to Saint Petersburg's Duma, she gave an inspired speech for the right of Russian women to receive a higher education. Full of energy and determination, Kovalievskaya was never satisfied with her work alone, and was always looking for other problems to solve.

In January of 1891, Sofia caught a bad cold, but as usual she went on working and giving lectures. Her cold spread to her lungs, and within a few days the blossoming woman, who had just turned 41, died. This was a shock for the scientific world, especially in Russia, where Sofia represented not only a great scientist, but an activist for the equal rights of women.

Passionate, genuine, and open; daring and refined, Sofia had expected a lot from the world, and from herself. Her intelligence and talent had been broadly admired. The Swedish poet Fritz Lefler called her "a soul of fire and thoughts," in his poetry. Scientists named her Michelangelo.

ERNEST RUTHERFORD
(1871 - 1987)

As one of those responsible for the birth of the radioactivity theory, he astounded the world with his discoveries in the field of physics. Ernest Rutherford created the nuclear model of the atom, and carried out the first nuclear reactions in the world.

A Grant For Life

The ancestors of the great physicist Ernest Rutherford were brave people. They left their native Scotland in the middle of the 19th century in search of a better life, and headed to the unknown world, New Zealand. In those days the British Company was recruiting new settlers for these wild islands, located thousands of miles away from Great Britain. The grandfather of the future outstanding scientist, a wheel master, was a determined man, and he decided that fate offered him a unique chance in New Zealand.

To get to their new land, the family had to go on a 7 month journey into the unknown on an old ship. The passengers stopped complaining about the lack of space after a terrible sea storm, and did not hide their tears when they saw a picturesque harbor on one of the islands of the New Zealand archipelago.

The youngest of George Rutherford's three sons, and the future father of the prominent physicist, James, almost never recalled this desperate journey. In his new country he became a farmer, and married Martha Thompson, one of New Zealand's first teachers. The newlyweds built their bungalow in the picturesque town of Brightwater, in the shadow of giant trees. There, on August 30, 1871, Martha gave birth to their fourth child, Ernest Rutherford. After Ernest, Martha gave birth to 8 more children, but it should be acknowledged that only one of her children was gifted with such extraordinary abilities.

Ernest finished his schooling with record results - he earned 580 out of 600 points for his grade. A considerable award of 50 pounds enabled the future scientist to continue his education. He entered the fifth grade in college, and professors immediately noticed the outstanding abilities of the new student.

His parents were very proud to read in his record book, "A very sharp and promising mathematician, ranking among the best students."

Ernest was an easy hand at the natural sciences and humanities. He won the highest awards and prizes for his success in physics, chemistry, English literature, Latin, and French.

The young man showed a particular aptitude for technical sciences. He was keenly interested in the working principle of various machines and mechanisms. Whenever he managed to get hold of an old watch, the boy would dismantle the entire mechanism with great pleasure, and he was always very disappointed when he couldn't manage to fix it, or assemble it again.

After graduating from college, the young Rutherford was accepted at Canterbury University in Christchurch, where he became seriously interested in precise and natural sciences. The future founder of new physics made his scientific presentation on the *Evolution of the Elements* when he was a second year student. Boldly he proposed that all atoms represented complex structures made up of the same elementary particles. At the time, such a proposal could be seen as a mere fantasy. Even though such a statement was a fantastic flight into the unknown future, the results of Rutherford's concrete research was realistic.

In a small shed with a cement floor, called by the students "the cave," he conducted experiments to research the properties of electromagnetic waves. At that time they were called "Hertz" waves, after the German scientist who discovered them. The 23 year-old researcher developed methods of identifying the electromagnetic waves, and used original instruments which he invented and constructed himself. Rutherford's first experimental research in this area was published in a student journal, where it greatly impressed students and professors at the university. Rutherford was famous among the students of Christchurch.

After graduating from Christchurch College in 1851, Rutherford was awarded a large, prestigious scholarship. Since the 1851 London World Exhibition, this scholarship was awarded only to the most talented graduates of provincial universities for the continuation of their education in England. The recipients could chose the university that they wanted to attend.

The good news reached Rutherford on his farm, where he was digging out potatoes. When his mother told him the unexpected news, the young man laughed. Throwing away the spade he said, "This is the last potato I am digging out."

He made the same journey his family had accomplished half a century earlier, not on a frail ship, but on an ocean liner. In New Zealand he left behind his parents, brothers, and sisters, and a fiancee, Mary Northon, a student of Christchurch University. She saw her beloved again five years later, and became his wife.

"Ready to accomplish a scientific revolution"

Cambridge University, and in particular the Cavendish Laboratory, were renown and acknowledged scientific centers. The Cavendish Laboratory had the reputation of being the Mecca of physics. Scientific stars of the first magnitude, and world-class scientists such as Maxwell, Raleigh, and JJ Thompson, headed the laboratory there at different periods, and conducted their research. Later, the young Rutherford described the years he spent in Cambridge as the threshold from the old to the new physics. The x-ray was discovered in 1895 by a German professor, Wilhelm Conrad Roentgen, and physics entered a new age. Student used to call Joseph Thompson "JJ," after his initials. As the director of the Cavendish Laboratory, a celebrated scientist, and a member of the Royal Society, Thompson was indeed a celebrity within the brilliant galaxy of Cambridge scholars.

Rutherford, feeling himself provincial, doubted that Thompson would take him as a practical researcher. However, the professor reassured him by telling him that he was approaching new problems in experimental physics, and he needed the energy of young and devoted researchers. Rutherford informed the professor in detail about his experiments conducted at the University of Canterbury, and also showed him his radio wave receiver. This made a good impression on the professor. Thompson was focusing on a different field of physics, but without any hesitation he offered to support Rutherford in continuing his interesting experiments at the Cavendish Laboratory.

Rutherford began his experiments with great enthusiasm. He used his receiver to create other devices. After one year of colossal effort, the young researcher achieved impressive results. He established a radio link between the Cavendish and the Astronomy Laboratories of Cambridge University. Back in 1896, three kilometers was a huge distance for a radio transmission.

More than one hundred years have past since then. Today we are at the threshold of the "information age" with the internet, and fiber, and satellite communication, but we should not forget that the basis for their functioning lies in a principle discovered by Rutherford.

Later Thompson confessed that Rutherford's successes in the field of radio signals was so great, that he "felt himself guilty" for convincing Rutherford to work on x-rays. However, further research on electromagnetic waves was necessary to improve and modernize the equipment for the receiving and transmission of radio signals, and Rutherford was not very interested in this type of problem. His mission in life was to be at the spearhead of research in new physics.

During Rutherford's time, the physics of the 20th century was being conceived. Even today, we cannot help admiring this remarkable period in history, when discoveries were made one after another in the fields of electricity, and composition of substances.. The x-rays that had just been discovered, were helpful in experiments made by Thompson, who discovered the electron, and created an electronic model of the atom. Rutherford participated as much as possible in the experiments of his professor. They achieved outstanding results together, in the area of the ionization of gases under the effect of electrical discharges and x-rays. Within 3 years of working with the maestro of physics, Joseph John Thompson, at the Cavendish Laboratory, Rutherford found outstanding results in his research. Immediately he was famous within the scientific circles of Europe and America.

The most important research, of course, was conducted on the radioactive properties of uranium and thorium. These experiments laid the groundwork for future activity in the field, and helped explain the most intricate processes taking place in the atom and the atomic nucleus. Soon, Rutherford received an invitation to take a position as professor of physics at McGill University in Montreal. When Peterson, the president of McGill University, came to Cambridge, Thompson personally introduced him to his student, Rutherford.

JJ Thompson said in his recommendation for Ernest: "I have never met a young scientist with such an enthusiasm and ability for original research as Mr. Rutherford. I am sure that if selected, he will create an outstanding school of physics and mathematics in Montreal. I would regard the institution that confirms Mr. Rutherford as professor of physics as a lucky one." At that time the candidate was only 26 years old.

Triumph in Montreal

McGill University was founded with the money left by McGill, a sponsor from Scotland. Back in Scotland, McGill was a hired farm worker who was tired of hopeless poverty. Like Rutherford's ancestors, he decided to try his fortune abroad. In Canada he showed an extraordinary determination, enterprise, and courage, and fate rewarded him. However, at the end of his life, McGill remained illiterate. His passion for knowledge remained deep in his mind, and one day it came out with his decision to invest a large amount of money, 40, 000 pounds, in the establishment of the first college of Canada. The college became McGill University.

The university had many other sponsors and supporters later on who contributed to its construction. The tobacco trader, McDonald, granted the university 4 million dollars. The people who gave to the university trusted in science and progress and spared no means on training its champions, without, of course, forgetting about themselves. The university departments were named after their patrons. Thus Rutherford, who chaired the physics department, was called "McDonald professor," and he did not view this as shameful.

Rutherford worked in Montreal from 1898 to 1907. It was a period of great enthusiasm for young scientists. In 1899 the Philosophical Journal published Rutherford's research paper. In the paper he spoke for the first time about particles ejected by radioactive elements. In 1900 he achieved a new success. He discovered the phenomenon of spontaneous emanation of thorium. This was the discovery that became the basis of nuclear physics. The research accomplished by Rutherford during this period, jointly with British chemist F. Soddy, demonstrated the process of transformation of one element into another. The physicists of McGill University called such transformations "modern alchemy".

The brilliant duo, Rutherford and Soddy, became the jewel of McGill University. The young scientists were motivated by a passionate desire to increase and enrich human knowledge about nature through their service. Later, Rutherford, who became the Nobel Prize winner wrote, "We were very close friends, and have remained so. The hours we spent together on various radioactivity experiments and tests have been feverish hours, but they have also been the most interesting and pleasant hours of my life."

The genealogical trees of radioactive substances, published in 1903, can be considered the main result of the Rutherford-Soddy collaboration. At that time, Marie Curie was defending her doctoral thesis, *The Study of Radioactive Substances*. Scientists of two continents were completing two important phases of the same research, at the same time.

Within a few years, Rutherford created an excellent environment for serious research work in physics at McGill. Thanks to his titanic efforts, the modest department of physics there turned into a world famous school for research in radioactivity. Rutherford's student, professor T. Allibon, wrote the following about his professor: "within a few years he got to the bottom of the entire complexity of radioactive transformations of elements, proved that radioactivity is the result of intranuclear transformations, and established that the energy of the ejected particle is supplied by the internal energy of the atom, because it is a million times the energy released during chemical disintegration." Rutherford discovered that the internal thermal heat of the earth is generated mainly by the radioactivity of minerals.

During Rutherford's time in Montreal there was a remarkable event in his life. In 1900 he went to New Zealand, where his parents and fiancee were waiting for him, and married his fiancee.

During all the years he spent in Canada, Rutherford maintained close contact with the scientific world of England. In 1905, at the age of 34, after his election to the Royal Society, the scientist was awarded with the Rymford Medal for his outstanding scientific achievements. In spite of his well organized laboratory and his work at McGill, Rutherford never stopped thinking of returning to England. After fulfilling his scientific mission, the young but acknowledged professor left Canada and moved to Manchester with his wife Mary and their six year-old daughter.

A Tiger in a Physics Laboratory

The second takeoff of Rutherford's research career belongs to his Manchester period, from 1907 to 1919. In 1907 Rutherford took up the chair of professor of physics at Victoria University in Manchester. William Kay, who was fortunate enough to assist the notorious scientist in those years, wrote about Sir Rutherford's shocking habit of running up several steps at a time when going up the stairs. The behavior of the young professor, who had just turned 36, did not match the solemn status of a Manchester professor.

Compared to his predecessor, the elderly and imposing professor Arthur Schuster, the youthful Rutherford looked like a boy. He appeared more like an athlete or a farmer - always rosy, and cheerful - than a professor. Once the Minister of Education from Japan, Baron Kikuchi, visited Rutherford's laboratory. Rutherford took a tour of the laboratory with the Minister, who was also a renowned physicist. Later, Kikuchi asked Schuster, who was the professor that guided them, if the man in the lab was not the son of the well-known professor Rutherford. Baron Kikuchi was quite astonished when he heard the answer to his question.

Rutherford's work at Manchester University helped to create a new field in physics. As a result of their determination, Rutherford and his contemporaries managed to unveil the secrets of nature. Rutherford and the German physicist Hans Geiger conducted extensive studies together in the field of particles, using the scintillation method (method of flashes). This research later brought sensational discoveries. Rutherford's co-workers said about him, "He possessed a lot of energy and enthusiasm. At work, Rutherford was like a tiger."

I see a sun in the atom nucleus.

In 1908 Rutherford was awarded the Nobel Prize for chemistry in Montreal, for his outstanding research work. This was the highest honor conferred to a scientist. The scientific world was not quite certain which field of science radioactivity was related to: physics or chemistry. Therefore, the Nobel Laureate gave the following title to the lecture he delivered in Stockholm: "On the chemical nature of alpha-particles of radioactive substances." At the age of 37 Rutherford became one of the youngest Nobel Prize winners. At the Royal banquet, the scientist jokingly said in his toast, "I have been dealing with remarkable transformations. However, the most remarkable transformation occurred when I instantly transformed from a physicist into a chemist." Later, after the discovery of the nuclear model of the atom, the new science was called nuclear physics.

In 1911 Rutherford became the first scientist to work out the planetary structure of the atom. This year marked the birth of the new physics. The planetary model contradicted classical electrodynamics, since according to classic models, the electrons must constantly shed their kinetic energy by means of radiation. However, the experiments on the scattering of particles made by Marsden, Rutherford's student, unequivocally predicted the existence of a heavy nucleus at the center of the atom. Rutherford clearly visualized the collision of particles, and even the apparent contradiction of his theory with the fundamental laws of electrodynamics did not hinder its proclamation.

The atom, as suggested by Rutherford, was like a solar system in miniature. The positively charged nucleus acted like the sun, and the electrons carrying the negative charge acted as tiny planets, revolving around the nucleus as a result of electrostatic forces of high tension. In the beginning, Rutherford described his model as planetary.

In 1912 the young Danish physicist, theorist Niels Bohr, began to work with Rutherford in Manchester. He was doing theoretical research on the stability of Rutherford's model for the atom. As early as 1913, Bohr successfully developed a theory for the structure of the atom on the basis of the quantum theory of light, which was yet taking shape at that time. This theory was in complete agreement with Rutherford's planetary model, and it also quantitatively explained the structure of spectra emitted by the atom. Consequently, the 20th century's prominent physicist, Niels Bohr, wrote an article called *On the structure of atoms and molecules*, and the Rutherford-Bohr model was developed further by the leading specialists of the quantum theory of mechanics, Louis de Broglie, E. Schroedinger, and W. Heisenberg.

In 1914 Rutherford was named Sir Rutherford, but that

was also the year that WWI broke out, drastically limiting the scientific work, and the personal plans of Sir Rutherford and his students. The Manchester group soon disintegrated. Henry Moseley, one of Rutherford's most brilliant students, was killed in the war, but before that, at the age of 23, he had made a name forever in the field of x-ray spectra studies. James Chadwick, the future Nobel laureate, was in a concentration camp, and Marsden was fighting in France.

Rutherford was called on to develop acoustic methods of spotting submarines, but he was always striving to make time for his own scientific work. When the war was over in 1917, the scientist started experimenting on nuclear fission and artificial transformation of elements. The idea, even though it seemed unrealistic, was not viewed as hopeless, because it was based on the results of previous experiments. Intuition had never let Rutherford down. In 1919 Rutherford was offered a position as professor and director of the Cavendish Laboratory of Cambridge University. The offer to become the head of the laboratory where he began his scientific career was too tempting. "He could do nothing but to take his place in the brilliant galaxy of the Cavendish professors," wrote Bohr.

The Golden Age of Cavendish

Rutherford became a Cavendish professor at the age of 48, and until his last days he conducted his research at Cambridge. Rutherford represented the great Cavendish school, which soon became the epicenter of the world's physics. He also became the president of the Royal Society.

The English proverb "a cat is not forbidden to look at the king" very accurately described the atmosphere of Cambridge in the 1920's. Back then, an entire constellation of "kings of science" worked at Cambridge. Those eminent, and at the same time very simple and nice people, were the mathematicians Dirac, Hardy, and Taylor, the biochemist Holland Hopkins, the poet Huysman, the philosopher Wittgenstein, the physicists Edington and Rutherford, and many others. The "cats" were the graduate students who intuitively felt that within the walls of this privileged institution, history was being made before their eyes. The students worked very hard. Their education in Cambridge was based more on the inspiration of the personal example of the "kings," than on learning the rules. The students had a real opportunity to learn from great scientists. Therefore, on the intellectual plain, the "cats" were slightly arrogant.

So were the students of the Bauman Institute of Technology in the Soviet Union. There was something in common in the academic atmosphere of Cambridge and the Bauman Institute.

The 1930's marked the "golden age" of the Cavendish laboratory. It was a time of exciting scientific discoveries. The young researchers Cockroft and Wolton were the first to find results for the nuclear fission of atoms by accelerated protons in high voltage accelerators. In his lecture on the structure of the atom, Rutherford predicted the existence of a neutral nuclear particle, right before his student, James Chadwick, discovered it experimentally and called it a "neutron". This discovery was a sensation because the intuition of the teacher had been proved by the experimentation of his student. In 1932 the young physicist and experimenter Patrick Blackett, discovered the positron.

The Russian scientist Piotr Kapitsa also worked in Cavendish during its "golden age". He was an excellent co-worker, a beloved student, and a friend of Rutherford's. Kapitsa worked in Cambridge for 13 years . In 1933 he was directly involved in the construction of the Mond laboratory in Cambridge, which was created specifically for him. The Mond laboratory is still doing very substantial research in the field of low temperature physics. Kapitsa was the first director of the Mond.

"The opening of the laboratory is the culmination of my aspirations for the last decade," said Rutherford at the opening ceremony. Kapitsa justified the aspirations of his teacher by making outstanding scientific achievements.

A Genius Crocodile

Rutherford was fond of making "excursions" to the laboratories of his students. He took a keen interest in their work, even if it did not relate to the subject of his own research. Everybody could anticipate his arrival at the laboratories because his booming voice could be heard from quite far away. In laboratories that used Geiger counters, which are very sensitive to any sound, there were special boards which read: "Keep quiet please." Everybody knew that this note was addressed to the good-natured, but loud Professor Rutherford.

Rutherford's students and co-workers called him "crocodile". It was said that this nickname was given to the respected professor by Kapitsa, who compared his teacher with a character from *Peter Pan,* a children's play by the British writer James Matthew Barry. In the play, Peter Pan is a boy who lives with his friends in Never Never Land. The children are all afraid of a wicked crocodile in Never Never Land, until one day it swallows an alarm clock. After that a loud ticking signals its approach. The "crocodile" in Cavendish could be angry at times, but his temper would always cool down soon.

I am not a physicist, but I like physics very much. I enjoy reading about the life and work of great physicists, and about their fundamental discoveries and achievements.

I always recall with enjoyment the excitement brought to me by my "crocodile," professor and physicist Struve. He became the victim of historical injustice and spent many years in Stalin's camps. He knew the real value of decency, honesty, humanity, and education. His lectures were astonishing because of the harmony of their content, the originality of their language, and their bright and unforgettable examples. Before lectures, students would literally fight for the front seats. He was very eloquent, and when explaining the properties of the membrane, the professor would even sing like a coloratura soprano. (He was an excellent singer.) He would also impersonate an electron, and explain the "screwdriver" rule by showing us how to open a bottle. It is clear that he did all of this in order to keep us students "warmed up". He was doing his best to help us understand the most critical points of physics.

I was fond of watching Struve test students. He was very happy when he received correct answers, but if he heard some nonsense he would burst into laughter. When a student was daydreaming the professor was very understanding of incorrect answers, but when there was no reason, he would become furious. However, there was so much wisdom and kindness in him, that nobody really feared him.

Ernest Rutherford, the famous physicist and director of Cavendish Laboratory, member of the London Royal society, winner of the Nobel Prize in chemistry, and Honorary member of many world Academies and Institutes, had more than an easygoing attitude toward all of his titles. When in 1912 he was knighted and conferred the title of Sir, his response to a congratulations was to joke that he had not requested such encouragement, and he hoped it would not sway him from his scientific work.

A sense of humor never abandoned this outstanding man.

He was quick witted, knew how to crack a joke, and understood humor. A good joke could make him laugh so loudly that his roar would "deafen" the people around him. He jokingly said about theoreticians, "they manipulate their symbols, and we in Cavendish explain real facts of nature." Once, the scientist was asked how he managed to stay on top of the wave of discoveries all the time. He burst into laughter and said, "I create those waves myself."

Rutherford taught Kapitsa to lecture at the Royal Society. "Show few slides, because when it is dark people leave the room," he said. Piotr Kapitsa recalled about his great teacher, "His sincerity and relaxed manner when dealing with people were striking. His answers have always been short, clear and precise. It was quite enjoyable to spend time in his company....One could bring up any problem with him, and he would willingly start speaking about it." Hating war and violence, the scientist was horrified by the atrocities of the Nazis, who in 1939 deprived many scientists of working in their homeland. The refugees included Albert Einstein, Max Bjorn, James Franz, Otto Stern and many others. In order to raise funds for these refugees, Rutherford created a Council for Academic Support in England. At the Council, he spoke about the need to save these refugees, as they were bearers of knowledge and experience which would otherwise be lost from the world.

However, financial support was not enough for the victims of Hitlerism. They needed help moving from Germany in such a way that their departure would not raise suspicion. Rutherford personally sent them invitations to lecture in Cambridge, and helped many move out of Germany. Among the people whom Rutherford helped to move out was Fritz Gabber, the inventor of a poisonous gas that was used by Germany during WWI. Rutherford refused to meet with that man, saying that scientific discoveries should not be used for war. What would this idealist scientist say if he had lived until the bombing of Hiroshima and Nagasaki?

People who work too long and think too little are foolish.

Be it in Montreal, Manchester or Cambridge, Rutherford was always surrounded by his bright, young students. Niels Bohr said that they were attracted "by his extreme possessiveness as a physicist and his rare capability as organizer in a scientific community." They were also drawn to his unusual enthusiasm, love for science, and sense of humor.

Kapitsa remembers that Rutherford took exceptional care of his students. He did not allow them to work in the laboratory after 6 o'clock, and he did not allow them to work on weekends at all. "It is quite enough to work until 6 in the evening. For the rest of the time people should think. People who work too long and think too little are foolish," he told Kapitsa.

According to another student, Rutherford would never withhold his ideas from his students. Many of the works that bear his student's names actually belong to him. He never suppressed a student's initiative, and always thoroughly analyzed and discussed the results with them, demonstrating an unlimited interest in everything.

Ernest had other interests besides science. He was fond of travelling, and a good athlete. In fact, he was famous as a sophisticated golf and cricket player. The renowned scientist valued human socialization most, and he liked creative, original and out-of-the-ordinary people. Rutherford not only had a scientific intuition, he also had a remarkable ability for spotting talent. This explains the fact that most of the teacher's students became major scientists.

Rutherford radiated generosity, and was always ready to help. In exchange, his students gave him their admiration, trust and devotion. His influence was as doubtless as the influence of the sun on planets. Professor Rutherford at the Cavendish laboratory was a center of ideas, and a source of light, warmth and life.

The teacher would often say the following to his students: "Do not forget that many of the ideas of your boys will be better than yours. You should never be jealous of the successes of your students...."

"Although that is not easy, as the years pass," he once confessed to Kapitsa.

The sudden death of Rutherford on October 10, 1937 took everyone by surprise. An illness had been destroying his health for a long time, but the news of his death still shocked his students.

Today, Rutherford lies beneath a modest gravestone in Westminster Abbey. Ernest Rutherford's name is associated not only with major achievements in modern physics, but with the qualities of an authentic scientist. Rutherford was a talented experimenter and researcher; a person of high morals, bold imagination, and original thinking; and a person with the ability to prepare successors.

One of them, P. Kapitsa, had every reason to say, "People like Rutherford are not the pride of just the nations in which they are born in and work in. They are the pride of the whole of humankind."

SRINIVASA RAMANUJAN
(1887 - 1920)

The brilliant possessor of mathematical talent, and Indian self-made man, made a sensation in Cambridge at the outset of the 20th century. Famous scientists were astonished by the results that he had achieved on his own.

He Went Alone

On December 22, 1887, a boy was born in a remote village of south India, who became a prominent mathematician of the 20th century. The history of science knows very few scholars whose original talent and tragic fate could compare to Ramanujan's.

He lived for 33 years only. The tragedy of Ramanujan is not only in the circumstances of his life and his untimely death, but in the fact that such an extraordinary and brilliant genius could not make proper use of the whole wealth of mathematical knowledge accumulated by human kind. He was self-taught. That means that he had to make his own way to mathematical truths. Ramanujan can be called a mathematical Paganini, with the only difference being that Paganini, when he was a child, was forced to practice playing the violin to the point of exhaustion, and Ramanujan was never forced to study mathematics. On the contrary, his religious parents were not happy with his interest in mathematics. Moreover, the young man never met anyone who could supervise his research and acknowledge its significance until he turned 27.

A school boy solves math problems for university students.

His parents belonged to the privileged class of Brahmins, but were poor. Ramanujan's father was a bookkeeper in a small textile shop in the town of Kumbakonam, in the Madras province. Ramanujan's mother was an extraordinary and strong-willed person, but her religious prejudices did not allow her to encourage her son's mathematical aspirations. She was unable to appreciate his talent and his inner world. With a strong hand, she guided her son along the only true path she knew. She wanted him to become a small clerk. This placed Ramanujan in a serious dilemma, which left its trace on his whole scientific career. His genius helped him ultimately to become a creative mathematician who entirely dedicated himself to his favored science, but that did not happen soon. In fact, it happened too late.

At the age of five Ramanujan was sent to a two year pre-primary school, after which he entered a primary school in Kumbakonam. He was always the best student, and surprised everyone with his good behavior and fine manners. Even more surprising, as a 4th grade student he independently studied the whole course of trigonometry in a two-volume textbook by Loney, which he borrowed from his acquaintance - a student of Madras University. The student was amazed by the schoolboy's knowledge in trigonometry, and quite often asked for his help in solving math problems.

When he was a fifth grader, Ramanujan independently discovered the already known formulas of Euler, but when he learned from his student friend that the formulas had already been discovered a long time ago, he hid his writings in the attic of his house. This was his first encounter with Western mathematics. The inquisitive schoolboy became a permanent visitor of the Kumbakonam library, but the library was deficient, and Ramanujan's command of English was limited.

The Magic Book of Carr

It was in 1903, when Ramanujan was a sixth grader, that he first found the only book in Kumbakonam by Carr, *The Collection of Elementary Results of Pure and Applied Mathemat-*

ics," published in London in 1880. The two-volume book contained over six thousand theorems and formulas, provided in a majority without proofs or conclusions. The book seemed like fate to the schoolboy. He became involved in proving formula after formula, grasping theorems, and trying to improve on common equation solving methods. A new world opened before young Ramanujan, and he devoted himself to it completely. Passionately he buried himself in this mathematical world, and found a happiness in his creativity, and a trust in his own intellectual strength. Since he did not have any other sources, every proof he made was the result of his own independent research.

He began with methods for building mathematical "magic squares." Then his attention was caught by geometry. After he became bored with this science, he involved himself with algebra, and independently discovered several new laws. He achieved all of this when he was just a sixth grader. Carr's book, as well as many other books, would probably have been consigned to oblivion, had they not been used by Ramanujan. Later, those books were scrupulously analyzed by prominent mathematicians, who tried to find out which ideas Ramanujan took from them. A well known professor of Cambridge University, Harold Hardy (1877-1947), gave the following assessment of Carr's textbook: "In general if we look at the book as a manual for a boy with such talents, the textbook is not bad at all. Ramanujan's perception of the material was amazing."

The young talent was only 16 when he finished school, and entered Madras University. For his academic success, he was granted a special scholarship for students excelling in the English language and Mathematics. The scholarship came at the beginning of his college career, when everything was so exciting and interesting for him. Universities, however, teach prepared materials, and do not always encourage student's aspirations. The professors looked suspiciously at Ramanujan when he knew better ways of solving problems then they did.

In the beginning Ramanujan always had a ready answer, but soon he lost his interest in learning. His studies were neglected. He devoted all of his time to mathematical research, and wrote his results in his notebooks, which later became widely known. (They were published in India in the form of photo-reproductions in 1957.)

At this point a series of misfortunes lasting 10 years began in the life of Ramanujan. He was unimaginably poor, and was forced to leave his school and wander. His attempts to get a job and continue his education ended in failure.

On the positive side, he continued his independent studies in mathematics, and fell in love with a girl. In 1909, Ramanujan got married.

A Post Office Clerk and the Great Hardy

In 1910 Ramanujan wrote the famous Indian mathematician, Ramasvali Ayar, the founder of the Indian Mathematical Society, about his work. Professor Ayar looked at Ramanujan's notebooks and understood that he was a person of extraordinary abilities, although he did not realize the whole magnitude of the talent of the young self-taught mathematician. Ramanujan was introduced to an influential executive, Ramachandra Rao, who played an important role in his life.

The kind hearted Ramachandra used all of his influence to support Ramanujan's life and promote his scientific career. In the beginning, he supported him with his own resources, but later, seeing that Ramanujan was burdened by such a position, he arranged for Ramanujan's employment at the Postal

Department of Madras. There Ramanujan was paid 30 rupees per month. Such a salary was, as the mathematicians say, a minimum/minimorum, but Ramanujan was too busy with other things to worry about postal work.

In 1913, thanks to the interference of the great mathematician Hardy, hope showed up in Ramanujan's life. In his first letter to Hardy Ramanujan wrote, "Dear Sir, I am an accountant clerk at the Madras Postal Department with a salary of only 20 pound sterling per year. I am currently 23 and I have no university degree. Since leaving school I have been doing mathematics in my leisure time. I did not follow the orderly training system that is offered at the universities, but I picked my own path. I am especially involved with dissipating orders - with results that mathematicians call amazing." Then he laid out the results of his research in elementary and high school mathematics, and referred to Hardy's works. "In your book I found a figure that gives a very close result, and the possibility of an error is small. Please look at the attached papers. I am poor and cannot publish them myself. If you find anything worthy in the papers, please publish it. With my request for your forgiveness for the trouble I have given you, I remain, Dear Sir, sincerely yours, Ramanujan."

Hardy understood that Ramanujan was a mathematical genius, but Ramanujan's fate depended on his reaction to this fact. The Cambridge professor made known the outstanding results found by Ramanujan in his early works. He also pointed to the 120 important formulas Ramanujan had found, which many prominent mathematicians had been working on, including Laplace, Jacoby, Legendre, Bauer, and others.

Hardy wrote, "Imagine the first reaction of a mathematician professional who receives such a letter from an unknown

Indian clerk. All it takes is one look at the results to see that this could be written only by a mathematician of the highest class. The solutions must be correct, since, had they been incorrect, no one would have enough imagination to discover them...Ramanujan has never seen any French or German textbook, and his command of English is so poor that he would not have been able to pass a basic test. It is surprising that he could come up with such mathematical problems at all, since it took centuries for European mathematicians to solve these problems, and some of them are still not resolved."

In the meantime an extremely interesting mail correspondence started between Hardy and Ramanujan. The self-taught mathematician's exceptional talents were revealed more and more to the professor. As a result, Hardy prompted energetic efforts to find Ramanujan a scholarship and invited him to come to Cambridge. Ramanujan did not accept the invitation, mainly because of his caste prejudices. His mother was especially opposed to his travelling to Europe. The only thing Hardy could do was find Ramanujan a scholarship in India. As a result, Madras University granted him a special scholarship. As noted by Hardy, beginning from that day Ramanujan became a professional mathematician. Letters were flying from Europe to Asia and back. However, Hardy was not happy only with a mail correspondence, and he insisted on Ramanujan's coming to Cambridge. In 1914 Hardy sent his disciple, professor A. Nevil, to Madras so that he could lecture at Madras University, and make another effort to bring Ramanujan to England. He even addressed a memorandum to the Madras community that began with the words: "The discovery of Ramanujan's genius promises to become the most remarkable event in the mathematics of today." In other words, incredible efforts were undertaken to bring Ramanujan to England, and finally it happened.

Cambridge's Special Light

In 1914 Ramanujan left for the center of mathematical thought in the British Empire, Cambridge. Until the 20th century, Cambridge University was not among the largest centers of mathematics, but at the beginning of the 20th century the young mathematicians Hardy and John Littlewood became the honor and pride of Cambridge, thanks to their distinguished work in the field.

Ramanujan's first months in Cambridge were mainly devoted to eliminating his educational gaps in mathematics. Hardy, Littlewood, and other prominent mathematicians were shocked by the depth of his knowledge in some areas of mathematics, as well as by his absolute ignorance in others. Hardy wrote about the beginning of Ramanujan's career at Cambridge, "We had a person who could operate model equations and theorems of complex multiplication of incredible complexity, and whose expertise in the area of continuous fractions was unsurpassed - a person who independently figured out the function of the d-equation, and most importantly, the asymptotic members of the most theoretical and figure functions. At the same time, he never heard of double periodical functions, did not know about the existence of the Cosh theorem, and had a very vague understanding of complex variable functions." One can only presume that he was blessed with a code of incredible capabilities and talents called "God's spark."

All scientists agree that Ramanujan came up with his results, early and later, correct and incorrect, with an odd mixture of intuitive guessing, contemplation, and logical judgement. In other words, Ramanujan was recognized as an exceptional genius. The self-taught genius started actively collaborating with well-known scientists and mathematicians of England. Hardy and Littlewood briefed him about some modern problems of the theory of figures, and together they reached results, so far unsurpassed. They noted that without the genius of Ramanujan, they wouldn't have even suspected the existence of certain formulas, which played an important role in proving these results. That was late in 1913.

In 1914 the war broke out. Scientific life in Cambridge came to a halt. Littlewood was mobilized into the army, and on the laboratory door there was a sign that read, "Visitors are requested to keep quiet since the noise disturbs the work of the Honorable Sir Isaac Newton." Hardy and Ramanujan continued their research. Ramanujan was absorbed by mathematics. The main bulk of Ramanujan's work was published in Cambridge, either by himself or in co-authorship with Hardy. For his prominent scientific achievements, Ramanujan was elected into the British Royal Society, and became a professor at Cambridge University. He was the first Indian to attain such honors.

Back in India

In the spring of 1917 Ramanujan fell ill. In the beginning his sickness was not threatening, but gradually, because he was unaccustomed to the British climate, and had an improper diet (he was a vegetarian) - his health was ruined. He had a sick lung from birth, and his illness developed into a form of tuberculosis. He continued to work day and night, even then.

In 1919 Ramanujan decided to return to India to work, at least for some time. He went to Madras University, the college he had left so dolefully as a first year student, because of his excessive preoccupation with mathematics. Unfortunately, going to India was a mistake. If he had stayed in England, his illness could have been cured, but his wish to return home and see his relatives was too strong.

After bidding farewell to Hardy and his Cambridge friends, Ramanujan left for India. He arrived there in April 1919 in a very bad condition. Apparently the tiresome travel completely ruined his health. He spent three months in Madras, and later moved to Kumbakonam, the village where he spent his youth and first encountered mathematics. His health was diminishing quickly, but he wanted no medical care, and he worked in a rush over his last brainchild - the special cases of theta functions.

Ramanujan died on April 26, 1920 in Chatput, one of the suburbs of Madras. The news about his death shocked Cambridge. Soon Hardy initiated intensive research on Ramanujan's scientific legacy, ranging from his early notebooks, to his stimulating theta functions. Cambridge professor J. Watson began a thorough analysis of Ramanujan's work, and was involved in this work for several years.

Ramanujan's prominence as a remarkable mathematician, and the significance of his work, was appreciated by Hardy and Littlewood. Soon after Ramanujan's death, Hardy wrote, "His insight into algebraic formulas and transformations of infinite rows, was stunning. I can't think of any one who could be compared with him in this regard, except maybe Jacoby or Euler... The excellent memory, patience, and perfection of a calculator were combined in him, along with an ability for generalization, a feeling for form, and a capacity for the immediate adaptation of a hypothesis - which made an exceptional impression and put him above all mathematicians in the areas of his interest."

The genius of Ramanujan belongs to history. He created special areas of mathematics and opened new mathematical worlds for generations of European mathematicians. He also found areas whose existence his predecessors did not even suspect. Scholars and mathematicians can only analyze his works and admire his original mathematical imagination and intuition. At the same time, not a single mathematician can avoid a feeling of bitterness and pain when thinking of what could have been given to mathematics by such a brilliant mind, had it been exposed to education earlier. The genius of Ramanujan, even in his last days, was his fascination with the light of science.

KONSTANTIN KUZMICH YUDAKHIN

(1890 - 1975)

An outstanding linguist, author of the first Kyrgyz-Russian and Russian-Kyrgyz dictionaries, and translator and author of many verses of the Manas epic.

"A master of literature is a god on earth!"

Little Konstantin was born on March 31, 1890 in Orsk, to a family of farmers. His parents were fully literate. They could write and read perfectly, and loved to do so, which was rather unusual for their social class.

One year after his birth, the family moved to Kazakhstan, to Aulie-Ata (today's city of Dzhambul) in search of a better life. Konstantin's father, Kuzma, mastered few languages, but he was a skilled man, and it took him little time to find a job. He was put in charge of the mail station, and little Konstantin was brought up in the atmosphere of his rather unusual profession.

Usually at night Konstantin's mother read her little son a fairy tale by Pushkin. On very rare occasions, Konstantin's father had a few minutes of free time, and he read from Pushkin, hiding his smile in his beard.

"Who didn't curse mail station inspectors, who didn't have an argument with them?" he asked, looking mysteriously at little Konstantin. "Who, in a moment of anger, did not ask for the book of complaints in order to write about injustice, bad manners?" At this point, Kuzma moved his terrible eyes from the text, and laid them on his listeners. Then he continued, "Who does not consider them the lowest part of human kind, equal only to the dead, or to bandits?" At this point Konstantin's offended mother would throw her arms up and say, "Calumny!"

Konstantin's father ignored her attempts to stop him, and continued reading the classic text in a loud voice. "Let's try to be fair and understand their position, and have more compassion. What is a mail station inspector? A martyr of the 14th grade, limited by his grade for ever. Isn't that real servitude! No time to rest, day or at night. Travelers pour out all the problems of their journey on the inspector. If the weather is bad, the road is nasty, the coachman is stubborn, the horses bad - it's all his fault." At this point Kuzma, himself a mail station inspector, stopped and looked at his silent family. "Who else than the great Russian poet could give a better description if us?"

Indeed, it sounded as if Pushkin himself had visited the Yudakhin family, accepted a hot glass of punch to get warm, and awaited the horses that would take him to the next station. Konstantin's father continued reading, "Entering his poor house, a traveler looks at the father, reading his words..." At this point Kuzma beat his chest dramatically. "That's about me!" he said, before continuing in an inspired voice, as if speaking to an enemy, "the inspector is lucky if he can get rid of the unwanted guest quickly. If there are no horses available, he will experience terrible threats, and a wave of insults. He must run though the rain, the storm, or the freezing cold to escape the shouting of the angry traveler..." At this point Konstantin's father abandoned the text and turned his head to his listeners, his hair stuck to the perspiration on his forehead, and his eyes sparkling with tears.

"And this is how Pushkin depicts our brothers! He just plays with our souls, even though these are simple words...How is this possible?" asked the mail inspector, impressed by the art of the poet, and unable to find an answer to his question.

Little Konstantin remembered this family scene all his life. He understood that Pushkin was a master of language, or in other words, a god on earth! Of course, the little boy wanted to be just like the genius. Usually childhood dreams are mere dreams, but not in the case of Yudakhin.

Yudakhin wanted to grow up faster, and not only grow but study. His parents were not opposed to his intentions, as their progressive minds understood that the rank of a mail inspector - even though brightly described by Pushkin - was not suitable for their son. By the age of six, Yudakhin had read all of Pushkin's work many times, and he knew all the fairy tales by heart. By the age of ten he had mastered not only Russian, but Kazakh, Kyrgyz, and Uzbek, thanks to his father's position. There were all kinds of visitors, and as a young man Konstantin helped his father to "conduct state tasks" such as greeting and taking care of guests, chatting, and writing reports. He never made a mistake.

Yudakhin finished at the local school and graduated from the institute of Aulie-Ata. He studied well at the Pedagogical Institute of Turkestan in Tashkent, and graduated a few years later as one of the best students. His first title was "national teacher," which he remembered proudly all his life, and his first mission was in the remote villages of Mankent and Karabulak, in Russian-Turkic institutes for Kazakh, Kyrgyz, and Uzbek students. The young linguist was fascinated by the language diversity, and he spent a lot of his free time doing research. He was successful at making the local populations literate, and at the same time, he noted down the local expressions, establishing similarities and differences between villages . He paid great attention to the oral culture, such as the tales, songs, and proverbs of the simple people. He understood that these things are the salt of a people!

As a young teacher, Yudakhin was the first Turkologist to become interested in gathering material about the Mankent and Karabulak dialects of the Kazkahs, Kyrgyz, and Uzbeks. He soon lost interest in teaching, and decided to focus all of his effort on the science of languages. He didn't even notice the beginning of World War I as he was busy studying Uyghur in Eastern Turkestan. His scientific knowledge became deeper, yet he wanted to know much more. In 1921 he entered the Oriental Institute of Turkestan, and his thesis, *The Karabula dialect as a model of non-Iranian northern Uzbek dialects*, became famous, even in Europe. The world famous linguist Polivanov praised Yudakhin's work and advised his colleagues to assist the outstanding, self-taught researcher.

As a result, the son of the mail station inspector was invited to Leningrad State University for training on scientific research. The White Nights, and the architecture of the city, including the bridges, and the pier by the Neva river where Pushkin himself used to walk, made the city like a fairy tale. The young scientist was overwhelmed. He understood that this was probably the best gift fate could send him, and he tried not to take it for granted.

Greatly inspired, he started working with even more energy. He gave a report on Uzbek dialects, which was praised by the members of the Scientific Council of the Leningrad Institute of Living Oriental Languages. His fame grew, and the Moscow Institute of Oriental Studies invited him to be a professor and teach. Yudakhin felt sad to leave the "northern Palmyra," the city of his childhood fairy tales, but he could not refuse the offer. He needed to develop his work.

In 1927 he wrote a dictionary of modern Uzbek, which was printed in Tashkent in the reformed Arabic alphabet. This book remains the basis of all Uzbek-Russian dictionaries. The dictionary is accompanied by notes on folklore, and historical, ethnographic aspects. In 1936 Yudakhin edited the first Uyghur-Russian dictionary - a huge step in Turkic studies. However, it was the first Kyrgyz-Russian dictionary, printed in Moscow in 1940, that brought him world fame! This was the first ever lexicographic work on the history of the Kyrgyz language. Unlike other bilingual Turkish dictionaries, this dictionary was filled with a rich lexicography, including different styles, dialects, proverbs and expressions, and notes on Kyrgyz history and traditions. This book became a reference for all Turkologists.

During his entire life Yudakhin continued collecting more material for his dictionaries. In 1944, he left his secure position as a Moscow professor, and while the Second World War was still going on, he moved to Kyrgyzstan to be closer to his sources. He was greeted warmly by the scientific and pedagogical community.

Yudakhin was fascinated by the decoration of Kyrgyz yurts. "No wonder the son of Yraman Yrchi from the Manas epic sings about the strip of felt that covers the top of the yurt! One needs so much brilliant, inspired words and metaphors to describe it," said Yudakhin. Working closely with Kyrgyz linguist Kusein Karasev, he gathered material for his dictionaries all across Kyrgyzstan.

Yudakhin had a tremendous influence on Kyrgyz intelligentsia. For example, when translating the works of William Shakespeare and Pushkin into Kyrgyz, poet Alykul Osmonov often consulted Yudakhin for etymology. Contemporaries remember how popular Yudakhin was among Kyrgyz families during his journeys across the country. He liked the traditional Kyrgyz food, beshbarmak, drank koumiss, and appreciated the local crafts. His colleagues, Yunusaliev, Tabyshaliev, Batmanov, and others, claimed that Yudakhin considered Kyrgyz the oldest and richest of the Turkish languages. In those days he was even accused of "Kyrgyz nationalism."

Regardless of the weather, Yudakhin went to the mountains to talk with specialists on history and local traditions.

He listened to the elders - the aksakals - and noted down all of their expressions. Sitting on a goat skin, he noted down his discoveries by the light of a petrol lamp, and moved on.

Yudakhin did not like to work with translations, but he loved to work on original texts. The outstanding linguist, who was greatly admired and respected by the Kyrgyz people, remained very modest. "I am ashamed to call myself the author of the Russian-Kyrgyz and Kyrgyz-Russian dictionary - I owe so much to the people who helped me in this work," wrote Yudakhin.

I remember very well when in the spring of 1960 Yudakhin visited our school, with the famous writer Chingis Aytmatov, after releasing his work on the language of Yssykkul region. We were all very nervous, and even our calm teachers became jumpy at the idea of meeting the "apostle of literature."

Yudakhin's tan face and clear eyes still remain alive in my memory. The children asked him many questions, and they clapped their hands when Yudakhin started speaking in perfect Kyrgyz. I was shocked when I heard him using Kyrgyz proverbs, myths, and legends. The writer Aytmatov listened carefully to Yudakhin, and as a master of language himself, was fascinated by Yudakhins' love for the Kyrgyz language. I also remember that we asked Aytmatov to write a book on school students, and when he published *Early Cranes* we were all convinced that this remarkable work on school children during WWII was written because of us.

About Yudakhin's Kyrgyz-Russian dictionary, academician and Turkologist Yunusaliev said, "the dictionary was a lifetimes work," and according to Oruzbaeva, "the creator of such a titanic work enters national culture triumphantly, with his name written in golden letters."

Yudakhin was saddened that his Kyrgyz-Russian dictionary, printed in Moscow in 1967, contained only 40,000 words; he wanted to include 25,000 more. However the work was still declared incomparable, and was awarded the USSR State Prize. Yudakhin also wrote about the classification of Kyrgyz dialects. In 1959 and 1971, he edited *Aspects of Kyrgyz dialectology*, *Kyrgyz dialectology*. The Kyrgyz -Russian dictionary, printed in 1965, became a reference work in Turkology. Yudakhin also made a tremendous contribution to Kyrgyz literature when he translated the Manas epic into Russian, and edited many of its verses in Kyrgyz.

Yudakhin was devoted to the Kyrgyz nation and its culture. The scientist gave us a fundamental work, and we will always cherish his memory. Yudakhin was elected three times as the deputy of the Soviet Republic of Kyrgyzstan, and awarded the Lenin Prize of the Red Order. When he died at the age of 85, the Kyrgyz people paid their last respects to this scientist, linguist, and author of unique works of national importance, with tears in their eyes.

ISA AKHUNBAEV
(1908 - 1975)

Kyrgyzstan... Many prominent sons were born to this fortunate land, encircled by sky-scraping mountains, green pastures, and grasslands. The people of Kyrgyzstan will never forget their sons whose endeavors benefitted the country. Isa Akhunbaev was one of these sons.

Spring had come. A boy with a broad forehead was sitting on the bank of a warm lake, resting his cheeks on his hands, and looking into the depth of the blue water as he listened to the sound of the waves. The white foamy waves looked like messengers from the sky. The day was absolutely still, except for the sound of the waves whispering, "Isa!"

The boy lifted up his head, frightened by the whisper. Who had called him? There was nobody around him. Only the sheep were grazing nearby. Was it the call of destiny? The water from the lake splashed and shimmered around his legs.

Isa Akhunbaev served as a shepherd for wealthy people. He had experienced a hard childhood, suffering through hunger, bitter cold, wolf attacks, and humiliation. He had escaped to China, and then returned to a helpless situation in Kyrgyzstan, before he had to take up hard labor.

One event in the boy's joyless life had turned everything upside down in his soul. He could not forget the face of a woman who had died after a long and hard illness. At nights it seemed he could still hear her moaning. Witch doctors had tried to cure her, and relatives had spent days and nights by her bedside, but nobody could help. For Isa, the acknowledgment of a limit to human capability was the worst part of it all.

Why do people fall ill? Why do they suffer from illnesses? Why can't they get well and live happily together with their children? Why do children have to become orphans? Why? Why? Such questions tormented Isa. He was deeply upset by the sick woman's death, along with her relatives and children. Probably it was then that he conceived of the dream of becoming a doctor. "I will heal people," he said firmly, "I will learn how to cure them, so they do not die from illnesses."

This well meaning dream helped to create a future star of

Kyrgyz medicine, and an unsurpassed surgeon in his time.

In 1916, a tragic year for the Kyrgyz people, the Akhunbaev's fled to China, where they suffered inhuman deprivations and misfortunes, while wandering in a foreign country among alien people. When they finally returned home after much tragedy, Isa's love and devotion to his country was reinvigorated.

The moment that the Kyrgyz refugees, back from China, climbed to the top of the Ton Gorge and looked down at the beautiful blue lake, not one of them could suppress tears; the young and the old were crying. Among these refugees, Isa became overtaken with feelings of patriotism, and his resolve to be useful to his people and his country was strengthened.

Just imagine a boy who gets up at first light every morning, in winter frost and summer heat, and walks on foot from his native village of Tory Aigur to the Balykchy township - a journey of 20 kilometers - every day, only to attend classes at school. Akhunbaev continued the habit of waking up at first light, well into his adulthood. When he was a professor at the Medical University, he woke up at 4 o'clock in the morning in order to thoroughly prepare for his lectures.

On the whole, the life of Isa Akhunbaev could serve as a model for sincere, devoted service to science and country. Judge it for yourself: In 1925 Isa Akhunbaev moved, with a small backpack on his shoulders, from Balykchy to Bishkek. From there he moved to Tashkent in search of learning. It was here that his fondest dreams started coming true, for it was here that Isa entered the preparatory department of the medical college.

After graduating from the college in 1930, he continued his studies at the preparatory department of Central Asian University. During his student years Isa exhibited the skills of an organizer, and thanks to his talents and inquisitive mind, he was ahead of his fellow students in his studies. At that time, Kyrgyz commoners rarely became highly qualified professionals. Isa was the exception. He was never idle, and he never took days off. It seemed that Isa was not interested in anything apart from his studies.

Nonetheless, an incredible thing happened to him at the university that had nothing to do with his studies. He met a good looking girl who was also good tempered, and an excellent singer. The girl's name was Bibikhan. Isa had never met a girl more beautiful than Bibikhan. Soon she became his wife, his friend, and the happy mother of his children.

In 1935 Isa Akhunbaev graduated from the Central Asian Medical Institute, and later he returned to Kyryzstan where he was assigned as the doctor of the surgery department at the Bishkek City hospital. At first the working man was very happy. He wrote in his diary, "I have achieved my goal! I am a surgeon. Now my entire life is the life of my patients, my home is my hospital." Isa's first operation was of a minor significance for everyone around him, but it was a matter of life and death for him. Emotional excitement at the completion of the operation, which he could not show to anybody, a feeling of stunning happiness after he heard the words of gratitude from his patient and saw happy tears from the patient's parents and children, all contributed to the monumental significance of the experience for him.

"I saved a human life!" he thought. The young surgeon's first operation was successful, and he was sincerely happy. Later he would go on to save hundreds of lives from death. Soon Akhunbaev's name became legendary, and he became as trusted as God.

Being a scientist means being selfless.

Isa Akhunbaev was greatly respected, not only by his patients, but also by researchers. In 1946, he brilliantly defended his thesis entitled: *Appendicitis in Children*. The thesis was later published as a separate monographic research work. The main subject that Akhunbaev was interested in as a surgeon and a researcher was the problem of endemic goitre in the native Kyrgyz population. With characteristic persistence and mastery, Akhunbaev struggled to understand this dangerous illness. His scientific and practical work on the prevention of the illness brought excellent results. Taking the initiative from Dr. Akhunbaev, the Kyrgyz government introduced iodinated salt into Kyrgyzstan, in order to prevent goitre. Its incidence has fallen from 40% to 5%. Akhunbaev's research on this subject was summarized in his doctoral thesis, *The Endemic Goitre in Chyi Valley*. It was successfully defended in 1948. Isa Akhunbaev was appointed the rector of the Kyrgyz State Medical Institute, and in the same year he became the first Kyrgyz citizen to become a corresponding member of the USSR Academy of Science. He took the most active role in the creation of the Academy of Science of Kyrgyzstan in 1954, and became its first president.

The man who had saved his people from illness, rightfully became its torch bearer. An amazing industriousness, a readiness to devote himself entirely to the needs of his people, and an ability to find common ground with co-workers, inspired everyone's respect and admiration. His national fame seemed absolutely not to touch him. He remained simple and accessible to everyone, always ready to help at any moment.

He had enough strength to help many. Akhunbaev never rested on his laurels. He researched shock, anesthesiology, reanimatology, lung, and heart surgery, and he was invariably successful. Concerned that the Kyrgyz health system could lag behind in such an important branch of medicine as cardiology, Isa Akhunbaev, despite his elderly age, went with a number of young surgeons to Moscow. There he attended the Institute of Cardiac Vessel Surgery, founded by the academician A. Bakylev, in order to learn how to perform heart surgery.

He achieved his goal. In 1959 in the capital city of Kyrgyzstan, Frunze (now Bishkek), he became the first to perform heart surgery in all of Central Asia. The first heart surgery in the world was performed in 1886, by the surgeon Reno, from Frankfurt-on-Maine. In 1938 the academician A. Bakylev performed a similar operation in the Soviet Union.

Isa Akhunbaev performed his first heart operation on a young man from Frunze-Sharshenbek named Myrzabekov, who had been suffering from heart disease for many years. Twelve days after the operation the patient could walk on his feet again.. There was no limit to the patients words of gratitude for the surgeon. "I trust you like I trust a God, professor. You gave me a second life," he said.

After his first heart surgery was successful, there was a boom in the number of Isa's patients. There were people from all over the Soviet Union - Russians, Uzbeks, Kazaks, Dungans, Germans, and Ukrainians - coming to Kyrkyzstan to seek Akhunbaev's help. When they recovered from his surgery, they wrote him letters filled with gratitude and respect. Those letters are still kept within the archives of the world famous Kyrgyz surgeon.

One can tell a lot about Isa Akhunbaev's compassion and humanism, by his readiness to help those in need. The following is one specific case of this that is worthy of retelling:

Once, when Isa Akhunbaev was the president of the Academy of Science, he was on a vacation with his wife, Bibikhan Akhunbaeva. They went for a couple of days to the Issyk-Kul Lake. All of a sudden, the famous doctor fell ill. He caught a bad cold, and his body temperature rose to 39 degrees Celsius. Isa could hardly breath, and even his wife, an experienced therapist, was thrown. Soon she collected her thoughts, and began to nurse him back to health. Her patient's temperature finally dropped at midnight, and he fell asleep.

Suddenly there was impatient knocking at the door. A messenger had come from the neighboring village of Kaji-Sai because a patient in serious condition with a stomach ulcer had been brought to a village hospital, and there was nobody there to operate on him. There was not even a surgeon at the hospital. The people knew that Isa Akhunbaev was at the nearby village, and had decided to ask him for a help. As soon as the ill professor heard what was going on, he jumped out of his bed and started getting dressed. Paying no attention to his wife's attempts to convince him not to go, he went out into the darkness.

On the way to the hospital he had to lye in the back seat of the car because he felt so ill. His temperature rose to 40, but this did not stop the surgeon from working. He was at the operating table until morning, performing an exquisite stomach surgery. Only when the last knot had been tied on the operational seam, and the patient was on the 'life' side of a barricade, did the professor take off his surgery gloves, and faint.

He awakened only after he was given some liquid ammonia to inhale. Immediately upon waking he asked how the patient was feeling, and the confused physicians of the hospital asked, "Which one of you?"

I wish modern doctors had the same attitude toward their profession, and their patients! As I am writing these lines, it seems to me that Isa Akhunbaev's heart, born for the people, is still beating in unison with the hearts of the hundreds of patients that he saved.

I have mentioned only a few episodes in the life of the prominent Kyrgyz surgeon, Isa Akhunbaev. I could have told you much more about his organizational talents, his diverse gifts, and his high government awards and titles, but there is probably no award higher than the recognition of the people.

I wish we all lived like Isa Akhunbaev.

EUCLID

(circa 365 - 300 BC)

"There is no royal way to geometry."

Greek by origin, Egyptian by residence, and scientist by profession, Euclid lived in the year 300 BC, during the rule of King Ptolemes I, the "Living God of Egypt." Euclid was very lucky to live in this period. King Ptolemes was known for his curiosity. He treasured the loyalty as well as the level of education of his subjects. If someone knew more than he did, he provided them with food and accommodation in the palace. If leaders of other times and other nations had followed the example of Ptolemes, they would not have ignored hunger, poverty, and destruction.

The curious ruler expressed his desire to master the new and fashionable science called "geometry". As Euclid was the best mathematician in the entire kingdom, he was invited to the palace.

"Help me to understand your science," ordered the king.

King Ptolemes' thoughts, words, and actions were beyond question, so Euclid could not possibly refuse. He bowed his head as a sign of agreement and asked, "How much time does Your Highness want to spend studying this science?"

"I have little time," acknowledged the king, "state duties, like insatiable lions, swallow my day and even gnaw at my night. I do not sleep as a human being should. There are too many reports, punishments, wheat that hasn't been harvested yet, invasion of grasshoppers ...So you see..."

"I see," said the mathematician, bowing his head even lower, and saying with a deep sigh, "how can I serve you then?"

"Show me the simplest, easiest way to the heights of your science, and I will try to catch up," said the king with a tone indicating no possible protest.

"But there is no royal way to geometry!" exclaimed Euclid. His shoulders shook and his black eyes flashed with anger, meeting the eyes of the ruler like swords. The people around them expected blood to be shed.

King Ptolemes calmed down. He forgave the scientist for his words of outrage, to the great disappointment of the court's headsman. The enlightened king could dislike the mathematician, but he could not ignore his contributions. Euclid founded the school of mathematics of Alexandria, which had no equivalent in the world. Just for his 30 volume work on logic, he deserved to have a monument erected during his life. Of course it was not a habit to build monuments to geniuses in those days. What a shame, for Euclid's fundamental work was invaluable, as it laid the basis for practical mathematics. Euclid himself defined its value to humanity by naming it *The Elements*. What a prophecy!

The remarkable definition by Euclid of the simplest element of geometry, the point, was as follows: "one can draw a straight line from any point to any point...any limited straight line can be extended....one can draw a circle from any center at any distance." These, as well as other observations, built the first elementary encyclopedia of mathematics, Euclid's *Elements*.

With no twisted phrases, everything seems so simple! That is probably the reason why Ptolemes thought he could easily master geometry. All you have to do is to put the golden key in Euclid's magic padlock!

Euclid's *Elements* remained a best-seller for 20 centuries. The popularity of the work could be compared to the Koran and the Bible. *Basis* completed Euclid's work in the 18th century, giving the world the first encyclopedia of algebra and mathematical analysis.

How could the great King of Egypt, Ptolemes, imagine that he would be remembered thousands of years later as the king who was lucky enough to rule during the time of Euclid the mathematician?

Nothing is eternal; kings, queens, and rulers, come and go. Geniuses, unfortunately, are mortal as well. Only a book of genuine knowledge survives its creators, protectors, and opponents. It "survives to take roots forever," to make life easier for future generations.

Herein lies the wisdom of our lives.

BLAISE PASCAL

(1623 - 1662)

"Man is a mere reed - the frailest of all beings - but he is a thinking reed."

Playing Dice and Having a Toothache

What makes the difference between a real scientist and a simple mortal? The fact that regardless of the situation, he is always in a working mood.

He thinks.

"I can easily picture a man without hands, without legs, without a head...but I cannot imagine a man without thoughts; that would be a stone or an animal.....we must try to think properly!" proclaimed Pascal, addressing not only human kind, but also himself.

A scientist does not simply think. His life is a constant, productive effort of the mind. Starting in 1642, Pascal spent three years conceiving, building, destroying, and rebuilding his arithmetic machine. Until he was finally able to build a model "worthy of the King of France," the young Louis XIV would not pay him for it. The king could not count up to more than ten in his early years of rule, which is perfectly possible even without a machine. The Queen Mother, Anne of Austria, Cardinal Mazarin, the "great Counselor," and the Prime Minister, spent huge amounts of money for the machine, yet the young heir was unable to appreciate its value. When Pascal finally succeeded in his task, the king delivered a unique document to the patriotic scientist. It was called a "Privilege for the arithmetic machine". It was something like a copyright, which made Pascal the only person allowed to produce and sell the machine. This was an unheard of privilege. Not only was the arithmetic machine in constant demand, but people were making orders years in advance. The fashion for the "arithmometer" took Paris, and turned society upside down.

Pascal turned, overnight, into a famous scientist and a

party animal. The most illustrious families of France invited him for lunch, or for dancing and hunting parties. He immediately had to master the art of cards, the most popular form of night entertainment. Social life absorbed Pascal and seduced him. New friends were made.

Once one of them, an addicted card player, lost large sums of money and made an unusual request to the mathematician. Could the mathematician, protected by the king himself, calculate with his machine how many times one should cast a die to achieve the best possible results? Was that task possible for the genius of the 17th century, or did he have to wait a few more centuries? How many times can one rely on chance in such a serious matter as gambling? The friend was slightly drunk, and he thought he was only making a good joke. Surprisingly, Pascal accepted the challenge. The scientist took the joke as a mathematical problem and decided to solve it with his usual determination.

To think, he solved it without giving up any social event. Within a few days, Pascal made a mathematical discovery. Probability is measurable! By mere chance, another genius, Pierre Fermat, was involved in the same problem. He also solved it successfully. Pascal was overwhelmed when he heard of the success of his colleague. Each solved the problem differently. Fermat based his work on his own theory of calculation, whereas Pascal based his work on mathematical methods. Reaching the same result proved that both were right. It is high time that human kind acknowledged "Her Majesty Chance" and her role in the history of human discoveries.

On another occasion, a terrible toothache prevented Pascal from sleeping, so he did his work on cycloids, a curved line representing the path followed by a point on a circle. Eight days of insomnia turned into eight days of enthusiastic research that ended with a collection of incredible discoveries. When at last a dentist appeared in Pascal's office with a pair of pliers for the "ultimate tooth operation," Pascal's face was shining with a childish smile. The pain was gone.

Pascal was also a unique philosopher, who genuinely believed that, "An easy and simple life is the best philosophy." Words of wisdom indeed!

Bibliography

Altaev. Al. LENARDO DA VINCHI. *Petrozavodsk, 1966.*

Arago F. BIOGRAPHIES OF FAMOUS ASTRONOMERS, PHYSICISTS, GEOMETRICIANS, *v.1 SPB, 1859; v. 2 SPB, 1860; v. 3 SPB, 1861.*

Astafurov V. I. M. V. LOMONOSOV. *M., 1985*

Avicenna (Aby Ali Ibn Sina) THE BOOK OF KNOWLEDGE. THE SELECTED PHILOSOPHIC WORKS. *M., 1999.*

Baev K. L. CREATORS OF NEW ASTRONOMY. COPERNICUS, BRUNO, KEPLER, GALILEO, *1995.*

Belonuchkin B. E. KEPLER, NEWTON, AND EVERYBODY M., *1990.*

BENEVOLENCE. *M., 1993.*

BIOGRAPHIC DICTIONARY OF RESEARCHERS IN NATURAL SCIENCES AND ENGINEERING, *v. 1,1958; v. 2M, 1959.*

Bogolyubov A. N. MECHANICS IN THE HISTORY OF HUMANKIND.*M., "Nayka", 1978.*

BOHR NIELS. LIFE AND LABORS, *Col. M., "Nayka" , 1967.*

Chistyakov V. D. THE STORIES ABOUT ASTRONOMERS, *Minsk. "Vysheishaya Sbkola" , 1969.*

Chistyakov V. D. THE STORIES ABOUT MATHEMATICIANS. *The edition 2, corrected and amended. Minsk,1966.*

CLASSICAL PHILOSOPHY OF CONFUCIUS, v. 1. M. -SPB., 2000.

Cohan V. F. ARCHIMEDES. SHORT ESSAY ABOUT LIFE AND LABORS. M.-L 1951.

Confucius. THE LESSONS OF WISDOM. *Moscow-Kharkov*, 2000.

Confucius. POLEMICS AND ARGUMENTS. SPB., 1999.

Devyatkin V. T. LEONARDO DA VINCHI M., 1952.

Dobrovolskyi V. A. D'ALAMBER. M., 1968.

Dolgopolov I. MASTERS AND MASTERPIECES. V. 1. M., "*Izobrazytelnoe Iskusstvo*", 1986.

Golovanov J. K. "ESSAYS ABOUT SCIENTISTS" M., 1976.

Grebennikov E. A. NICOLAS COPERNICUS. M., "*Nayka*", 1973.

Guber A. LEONARDO DA VINCHI M., 1952.

Hollingsworth Mary. THE ARTS IN THE HISTORY OF HUMANKIND. M., 1993.

Ibn-Sina (Avicenna) SELECTED PHILOSOPHIC WORKS. M., "*Nayka*", 1980

Ishlinskyi A. J., Pavlova G. E. M. V. LOMONOSOV - GREAT RUSSIAN SCIENTIST. M., 1986.

Karyagin K. M. CONFUCIUS. HIS LIFE AND PHILOSOPHIC WORK. SPB., 1897.

Kedrov F. ERNST RUTHERFORD. M., "*Znanie*", 1980.

KOMSOMOLSKAYA PRAVDA, XII- 2000.

Kubis L. P. ERNST RUTHERFORD. M., 1958.

Kurie E. MARIA KURIE. *M., Atomizdat, 1967.*

Kydryavtsev P. S. FARADEI. *M., 1969.*

Lazarev V. N. LEONARDO DA VINCHI. *1952.*

Levin V. I. RAMANUJAN *M., "Znanie", 1968.*

Lishevskyi V. P. ANDREI PETROVICH MINAKOV. *M., "Nayka", 1983.*

Lishevskyi V. P. STORIES ABOUT SCIENTISTS. *M., "Nayka", 1986.*

Litvinova E. F. SOFIA KOVALEVSKAYA ZhZL. Bibliographic Library of Florentius Pavlenkov, *v. 35 (Reprinted Edition) Chelyabinsk, 1999.*

Litvinova E. F. D'ALAMBER AND HIS LIFE. *SPB, 1896.*

Livanova A. THREE DESTINIES. THE COGNITION OF THE WORLD. *M., "Znanie", 1969.*

Lomonosov M. V. THE FULL COLLECTION OF WORKS. 10 volumes. *M.-L, 1950-1957.*

Lurie S. Y. ARHIMEDES *M. -L, 1945.*

Malyavin V.V. CONFUCIUS. *M., "Molodaya Gvardia", 1992.*

Menshytkin B. N. THE BIOGRAPHY OF MICHAIL VASILIEVITCH LOMONOSOV. *M.-L, 1947.*

Mysskyi I. A. HUNDRED OF GREAT THINKERS. *M., 2000.*

Nezavisimaya Gazeta, *XII-2000.*

Orlovskyi Boleslav. THE ROW OF GREAT ENGINEERS. *NashaKsengarnya, Warsaw, 1980.*

Peltser A. WHO ARE YOUR PYTHAGORAS? *"Znanie-Sila"*, *1994*, #12.

Perelomov L. S. CONFUCIUS. LIFE, SCIENCE, FATE. *M., "Nayka", 1993.*

PHILOSOPHY IN ENCYCLOPEDIA OF DIDRO AND D'ALAMBER. *M. 1984.*

Polovenov Y. ESSAYS ABOUT SCIENTISTS, *"Molodaya Gvardia", 1970.*

Ramodin B. A. THE GREAT SCIENTIST OF CENTRAL ASIA IBN SINA (AVICENNA). *M., 1952.*

Rutherford - SCIENTIST AND TEACHER TO 100TH ANNIVERSARY SINCE BIRTH. *M., "Nayka", 1973.*

Sagadeev A. B. IBN SINA (AVICENNA). *M., "Mysl", 1985.*

Saldadze L. G. IBN SINA (AVICENNA). THE PAGES OF GREAT LIFE. *Tashkent, 1983.*

Samin D. K. HUNDRED OF GREAT SCIENTISTS. *M., "Mysl", 1985.*

Sartbaev K. K. KONSTANTIN KUZMICH JUDAKHIN. *"Turkic Studies" Frunze, 1970.*

Semenov A. A. ABY ALI IBN SINA (AVICENNA) *Stalinabad, 1953.*

Veselovskyi I. N. ARCHIMEDES. *M., 1957.*

Voloshinov A. B. PYTHAGORAS: THE UNION OF TRUTH AND

Yamvlikh THE LIFE OF PYTHAGORAS. M., 1998.

Zhmyd L. Y. PYTHAGORAS AND HIS SCHOOL. *Leningrad, 1990 .*

About the Author

Mairam D. Akaeva was born in the Talas mountains of the Kyrgyz Republic. She graduated from the Leningrad (now St. Petersburg) Technological Institute. As a professor she authored a textbook called *Theory of Mechanisms and Machines*.

Professor Akaeva's first book, *Stars of Science*, was published in India in 1995. In 1999 the Moscow publishing house, Sobesednik, published her book, *Archimedes and Others*, and in 2001 the same house published *Stars of Science*.

Mairam Akaeva is married to Askar Akaev , a renown scientist and academician who is now the President of the Kyrgyz Republic. She has four children.